Understanding Behaviour 14+

Understanding Behaviour 14+

Vicky Duckworth, Karen Flanagan,
Karen McCormack and Jonathan Tummons

 Open University Press

Open University Press
McGraw-Hill Education
McGraw-Hill House
Shoppenhangers Road
Maidenhead
Berkshire
England
SL6 2QL

email: enquiries@openup.co.uk
world wide web: www.openup.co.uk

and

Two Penn Plaza, New York, NY 10121-2289, USA

Open University Press 2012

A catalogue record of this book is available from the British Library

ISBN10: 0335237894 (pb)
ISBN13: 9780335237890 (pb)
e-ISBN: 9780335247325

Library of Congress Cataloging-in-Publication Data
CIP data has been applied for

Typeset by Aptara Inc., India
Printed in the UK by Bell and Bain Ltd., Glasgow

MIX
Paper from
responsible sources
FSC® C007785

FSC
www.fsc.org

The McGraw·Hill Companies

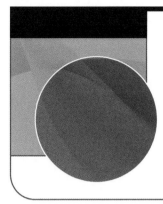

Praise for this book

"The effective management of the behaviour of 14+ learners has become a key issue across the school and lifelong learning sectors. The new Ofsted Schools, Common Inspection Framework and Initial Teacher Education Framework have behaviour management as a central focus. The raising of the participation age (RPA) will require teachers to manage the learning of a wider range of students in an increasingly broader spectrum of institutional contexts. Understanding Behaviour 14+ will be a welcome resource for these teachers, whether more or less experienced. The authors recognize that there are no quick fixes to deal with what are extremely complicated relations and situations and avoid a 'tips for teachers' approach to behaviour management. They emphasise the importance of understanding why students behave the way they do and, with an excellent blend of theory and practice, encourage teachers to use reflection and to take solution- rather than problem-based approaches to managing behaviour. The text is highly accessible and issues are practically grounded in real life case studies."

—*Andy Armitage is Head of The Department of Post-Compulsory Education, Canterbury Christ Church University, UK. He recently completed a year's secondment to Ofsted as an inspector of Initial Teacher Education.*

Contents

About the Authors

Vicky Duckworth is a senior lecturer and course leader for the full-time Postgraduate Certificate in Education (PGCE) in Post Compulsory Education and Training provision at and Schools' University Lead Edge Hill University, UK. She has published on a range of issues in the field of literacy, critical and emancipatory approaches to education, widening participation, inclusion and community engagement. She undertook her PhD at the Educational Research Centre, Lancaster University, the focus being 'Learning trajectories, violence and empowerment among adult basic skills students. Vicky's research interests continue to include practitioner and collaborative research methods, participatory action research and linking research and practice. She remains strongly engaged in exploring empowerment and egalitarian approaches to teaching and learning and violence in relation to learning. She is part of several national and international networks. She is co-author with Jonathan Tummons on a number of books and Steve Ingle of Enhancing Learning through Technology on lifelong learning: fresh ideas; innovative strategies.

Karen Flanagan, Education, Learning and Skills Directorate, Kent County Council. Karen was herself a mature non-traditional student and, since enrolling on an access course by chance, has embraced the world of education and the opportunities and choices it brings. She has worked in higher education, further education, alternative provision and local authority settings. Her current focus of work is with disaffected and disengaged students at Key Stage 4 who have been, or are in danger of becoming excluded. She is committed to working with vulnerable and marginalized groups in all settings and is particularly interested in the role education has in empowering individuals and groups.

Her other publications include: A. Armitage *et al.* (2011) *Developing Professional Practice 14–19* (Pearson Education) and A. Armitage *et al.* (2007) *Teaching and Training in Post Compulsory Education* (Open University Press/McGraw-Hill).

Karen McCormack is a senior lecturer and course leader on the Secondary PGCE Programme at Edge Hill University. She has taught for over twenty years in secondary schools and during that time her main areas of teaching were the 14–19 age range. Her experience of working with young adults has inevitably helped to develop her understanding of how the 14–19 age range learn and how best to teach and encourage learning and achievement in that age group. Current research includes how to plan outstanding lessons for Key Stages 4 and 5 and she has focused on the need for 14–19 students to feel ownership over their own learning and understand the relevance of what goes on in the classroom. She believes that creativity is an essential part of the 14–19 classroom and that, without genuine participation in an engaging learning environment, learning is likely to be mostly superficial.

Jonathan Tummons is senior lecturer in education and co-convenor of the education and work-based learning research group at Teesside University, UK. He teaches across both undergraduate and postgraduate provision. He has published widely on a range of issues related to learning, teaching and assessment in further, adult and higher education. His research has appeared in a number of leading academic journals, including *Studies in Higher Education, Assessment and Evaluation in Higher Education* and *Higher Education Research and Development.* He is the co-author, with Vicky Duckworth, of *Doing Your Research Project in the Lifelong Learning Sector* (in press) and *Contemporary Issues in Lifelong Learning* (2010) (both Open University Press).

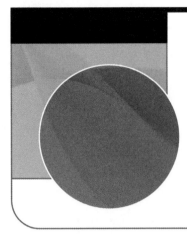

Acknowledgements

Vicky Duckworth: To my daughters Anna and Niamh, who never fail to inspire me. Also to Craig Ludlow for his wisdom.

Karen Flanagan: To my boys Callum and Jordan, simply for being themselves, I am so very proud of them. My partner Paul and my friends, especially Kay, for their support and laughter, my mum and finally all those teachers who are able to motivate and inspire students just like me.

Karen McCormack: Thanks to my family for their support and perseverance and the many students who have taught me so much.

Jonathan Tummons: As always – for Jo, Alex and Eleanor.

CHAPTER

1

Introduction: Behaviour and learning

The book is aimed at both experienced and non-experienced practitioners in the secondary and Lifelong Learning Sector (LLS). It identifies the importance of ensuring that learning environments are not hindered by challenging behaviour and how this can be a key area of development for practitioners across all sectors, ages and phases of learning. It is important to note that challenging behaviour is not the reserve of those with social, emotional or behavioural difficulties, and disaffection is not limited to the secondary sector. Actually, when one considers the numbers of interactions a teacher experiences in any day, perhaps the question should be why there are not more instances of unwanted behaviour.

We believe that in order for practitioners to be able to seize opportunities and optimize learning, they need to have the confidence and expertise to ensure that students actually do learn. We recognize and address the very real challenges faced by both trainee teachers and the most experienced practitioners in developing and implementing effective strategies for meaningful classroom behaviour management. This means having a sound understanding about effective behaviour management and how to incorporate this into the principles of effective learning and teaching. We offer a rich variety of practical skills and knowledge to put these principles into practice.

In the present educational climate of targets and outputs, practitioners are frequently pressured to increase academic performance of their students and can feel frustrated when they realize that, more often than they would like, they are forced to use their teaching time to manage problem behaviours. Indeed, because academic performance and behaviour are often connected, reducing challenging behaviours is likely to result in a more positive learning environment, which improves students' experience of learning and subsequently their academic performance. The application of your knowledge and skills in behavioural management can have a huge and powerful effect on the lives of your students.

Qualified practitioners and trainee teachers with high confidence levels define behaviour management in more positive terms. A point to remember is that even the most experienced teachers will have conflict in their classes. Despite the best prevention strategies, some students will be physically or verbally aggressive, and some will refuse to accept the consequences of that behaviour. According to these authors, the need to understand the uniqueness of students, empower them and involve them in all aspects of behaviour management in the classrooms cannot be overemphasized. To this end, disciplinary measures are not forced down the throats of students but instead emphasis is on teaching responsibility of, and accountability to one's modes of behaviour. We believe that that teaching should provide an environment in which the learning of new skills and knowledge takes place. This is best accomplished when students receive generous amounts of positive reinforcement for academic achievement. Furthermore, when a student is reprimanded or punished for misbehaviour, cessation of misbehaviour does not mean that the student is learning.

Behaviour is increasingly becoming an area for scrutiny and the new Ofsted framework for school inspection (Ofsted 2012a) makes this clear. The four key inspection headings are that of:

- quality of teaching;
- quality of leadership and management;
- behaviour and safety of pupils;
- achievement of pupils.

Inspectors are asked to make a judgement about students' behaviour in the classroom, especially that of persistent low-level disruptive behaviour, and over time through evaluation of sanction and rewards, fixed term and permanent exclusions, or repeated incidences of bullying (the issue is not the number of recorded incidents but the action taken and how effective the action has been (Ofsted 2012b)).

Behaviour is not so easily measured or evaluated in further education (FE) and training provider settings where many students who are disaffected can choose to vote with their feet. This can see students choosing not to attend lessons or, when they do attend, arriving late or/and leaving early. This can be demoralizing for the teacher as well as disrupting other students in the class. Proposed changes to the way in which these organizations are to be inspected have been published as part of a consultation on the changes to the Common Inspection Framework due to be implemented in September 2012. The Common Inspection Framework is used in the inspection of all providers who deliver education and training to those aged 16 or over, with the exception of sixth forms and higher education (HE); this includes work-based learning providers, Adult and Community Learning, Offender Learning and Next Step provision as well as colleges of FE. The new proposals have taken into account the changes in legislation and policy as reflected in the Education Act 2011 and significant White Papers such as the Schools White Paper, *The Importance of Teaching* (DfE 2010a).

The consultation proposes three headline grades, that of:

- outcomes for students;
- the quality of teaching, learning and assessment;
- leadership and management.

It also makes clear the need to evaluate the effectiveness of learner outcomes:

 We propose to judge outcomes for students by giving particular attention to how well:

- all students achieve;
- gaps are narrowing between different groups of students;
- students develop personal social and employability skills.

> • students progress to higher level qualifications, and into jobs that meet local and national needs.
>
> *(Ofsted 2012c)* 〝〝

Behaviour will be evaluated as part of equality and diversity through 'teaching, learning and assessment, and the behaviour and attitudes of students and staff' (Ofsted 2012c: 10). Many training providers have been used to providing employability skills and functional skills, often accessing funding which specifically focuses on groups such as those young people who are Not in Education, Employment or Training (NEETs). While FE has traditionally been a place of choice, and in particular to offer 'second chances' and vocational pathways, changes in culture and policy have led to forced participation for students who might, in previous generations, have been able to access viable employment alternatives to education or training at the age of 16 and 17. The lack of viable choices and progression can lead to disaffection and unwanted behaviour as a reflection of these structural changes.

It is important to remember that unwanted behaviours are exhibited in many forms and in many settings. This can cause problems for trainee tutors and qualified staff in terms of expectations and successful classroom management. For example, a significant number of applicants for post-compulsory pre-service Initial Teacher Training (ITT), when asked, 'Why do you want to work in the Lifelong Learning sector?' responded that 'They want to work with adults who are enthusiastic about the programme they have chosen', or 'Because they want to be there' (Wallace 2008). Thus, older students are perceived to be mature in outlook as well as age, committed and motivated. Expectations such as these are not only idealistic but also unrealistic.

The aim, and indeed challenge, of this book are not only to explore a range of possible reasons as to '*why* students behave in the way they do', but to uncover, reveal and engage the reader in meaningful self-evaluation and reflection, that will assist the practitioner to implement change within problematic relationships and environments. When someone mentions behaviour management, our first thought may be about controlling students or preventing inappropriate behaviours. We can expend a great deal of energy managing students so that inappropriate behaviours will not occur. This book hopes to challenge existing paradigms in order to break down barriers, and encourage professional responsibility and autonomy for promoting positive relationships instead of passive acceptance of unwanted behaviours and/or reliance on a culture of 'blame' (Parsons 1999). In doing so, the drive is to challenge labels which position students as failures and reduce motivation, self-esteem and aspirations. In the evaluation and consideration of difficult environments as opposed to difficult or 'bad' students, we are already moving from a deficit model and engaging in a process of change that will allow the practitioner to reflect in a far more constructive and objective manner.

The process of critical reflection and evaluation allows practitioners to acknowledge their own feelings in this process. While there are strategies that can help in a reactive sense to situations and behaviours as they occur, such as body language and proxemics (Hall 1966), there are no 'quick fixes' to deal with what are extremely complicated and complex relationships and situations.

This approach, while initially daunting, allows the practitioner to be freed of the shackles of 'labels' that are neither helpful nor constructive and instead becomes a powerful tool for transforming negative learning environments, with the emphasis on an active solution-focused approach.

Structural inequalities remain and stubbornly persist in the education system:

> 66 England had one of the highest gaps between high and low performing pupils and a strong relationship between social background and performance. 13.9% of the variance in performance of pupils in England could be explained by their social background, as compared to just 8.3% in Finland and 8.2% in Canada.
>
> *(DfE 2010a)* 99

Recognition of the gaps between students who do most well and those who do the least well has been reflected in the new Ofsted framework for school inspection and in the proposed changes to the Common Inspection Framework where the key focus is that of recruiting and retaining high-quality teachers. High-quality teachers are those teachers who are able to:

- engage students;
- challenge and inspire students; and
- ensure teaching allows all students to achieve their full potential.

These teachers are resilient, creative and inspiring and able to implement a range of strategies to support and promote teaching and learning in a range of situations. They are also reflective and look at education as a means to recognize and meet the needs of diverse students rather than limiting their expectations to homogeneous groups of students who live in fictional rather than real settings.

Throughout teacher training and on CPD (Continuous Professional Development) programmes, high numbers of practitioners ask for effective strategies for effective management of behaviour. A number of books offer a 'paternal' approach based on authority and power which fail to explore more holistic and meaningful engagement with students.

In contrast, this book challenges a deficit model to behaviour management which positions the learner as lacking, and instead provides the tools whereby practitioners can employ professional autonomy to engineer positive change. It recognizes that a main drive of the education system in a democratic society is to offer quality education for *all* students so that they can reach their *full* potential and contribute to and participate in that society throughout their lives. In doing so it places students at the heart of the text.

How to use this book

This book can be read from beginning to end or a chapter at a time: each chapter is designed to offer different insights and approaches, and, where necessary, links to topics covered in other chapters are included. Practical and theoretical issues are blended throughout the book but for those readers who are looking for particular themes, rather than planning to read through the book from the start, a brief summary may be useful:

Chapter 2 consists of a discussion of issues around behaviour of diverse groups of students in both the secondary and further education context. It draws on relevant research to explore behaviour management and touches on **labelling theory** and students' expectations.

Chapter 3 investigates possible reasons as to 'why students behave in the way they do'. This includes a range of sociological and psychological theoretical concepts including motivation, barriers to learning, the process and impact of labelling, attribution theory, attachment theory, an exploration of the medicalization model of SEN (special educational needs) and disability with a focus on Attention Deficit Hyperactivity Disorder (ADHD).

Chapter 4 focuses on the adolescent and provides an overview of development, in particular that of the brain and myelination. There is discussion of physiological and psychological changes, with a particular focus on identity and the need for adolescents to detach from adults in order to develop their own unique identity. It looks at the impact of emotional health on learning, considering disorders commonly associated with adolescence, e.g. eating disorders. It will suggest that 14- to 19-year-old students are indeed a distinct group owing to these dramatic changes and thus require additional understanding and planning in terms of relationships.

Chapter 5 focuses on adult students. It debunks the myth that all adult students are motivated and able to engage in independent learning. It explores common barriers to learning including negative past educational experiences and home environments. It also considers theories and issues of self-esteem and confidence and explores teaching approaches to building self-esteem. This chapter will also consider theories of adult students, including those of Maslow and Rogers, and explore the 'expectations' of both practitioners and students.

Chapter 6 considers models of reflective practice and why and how this is useful to the practitioner in terms of behaviour management. It then builds on these models to explore a solution-focused approach as well as the uses of CBT (cognitive behavioural therapy). The latter approach acknowledges that 'you think the way you feel' (Wilson and Branch 2006: 11) and introduces a combination of cognitive processes – your thinking, your feelings and your behaviours – including the way in which you react in situations and therapy. It shows how this approach can be used to combat the problems or issues by focusing on change, including consideration of the way practitioners may assign meaning to events and ways to avoid escalation.

References

DfE (Department of Education) (2010a) *The Importance of Teaching* (Schools White Paper). Available at: https://www.education.gov.uk/publications/ standard/publicationdetail/page1/CM%207980.

DfE (2010b) *The Case for Change.* Available at: https://www.education .gov.uk/publications/eOrderingDownload/DFE-00564-2010.pdf.

Hall, E. (1966) *The Hidden Dimension.* New York: Doubleday.

Hayes, D. (2004) The therapeutic turn in education, in D Hayes (ed.) *The RoutledgeFalmer Guide to Key Debates in Education.* London: Routledge-Falmer.

Ofsted (Office for Standards in Education) (2012a) *The Framework for Schoool Inspection.* Available at: http://www.ofsted.gov.uk/resources/framework-for-school-inspection-january-2012.

Ofsted (2012b) *Subsidiary Guidance Supporting the Inspection of Maintained Schools and Academies from January 2012,* No. 110166. Available at: http://www.ofsted.gov.uk/resources/subsidiary-guidance-supporting-inspection-of-maintained-schools-and-academies-january-2012.

Ofsted (2012c) Consultation Document: Common Inspection Framework. Available at: http://www.ofsted.gov.uk/resources/common-inspection-framework-2012.

Parsons, C. (1999) *Education, Exclusion and Citizenship.* London: Routledge.

Wallace, S. (2008) *Managing Behaviour in the Lifelong Learning Sector.* Exeter: Learning Matters.

Wilson, R. and Branch, R. (2006) *Cognitive Behavioural Therapy for Dummies.* Chichester: John Wiley and Sons, Ltd.

Zay, D. (2005) Preventing school and social exclusion: a French–British comparative study, *European Educational Research Journal,* 4(2): 109–20.

CHAPTER

2

Why should we include all students?

By the end of this chapter, you will be able to:

- critically explore issues around the behaviour of diverse groups of students in both secondary and further education contexts;
- link labelling theory to learner behaviour across the secondary and further education sectors;
- demonstrate an awareness of relevant research to behaviour management regarding learner behaviour and learner attitudes towards behaviour management

Introduction: expectations of behaviour

Many of the trainee teachers with whom I have worked and continue to work find aspects of their own students' behaviour surprising, challenging and unpredictable, irrespective of whether they are full-time trainees on placement, or part-time trainees who are in-service. This is not to say that trainees do not expect to encounter challenging or difficult behaviours: far from it. But it is where they find these behaviours that provides the greatest surprises and provokes the most challenging reflections and evaluations.

Let me explain in more detail, drawing on the histories of three trainees with whom I have worked in the recent past. The first of these trainees, Liz, had been recently appointed to a full-time lecturing post in a further education college and was studying for her Certificate in Education on a part-time in-service basis. She was teaching a range of courses (not in itself surprising), but with a particular focus on AS and A2 sociology, working predominantly with 17- and 18-year-old students. The second trainee, Kevin, was a full-time PGCE student and was on a placement in an academy school, teaching English and history to 14- and 15-year-olds. The third trainee, Robin, was also a full-time PGCE student and was teaching also 14- and 15-year-olds, but in a very different context: at a further education college, where the students in question were studying vocational and technical courses at Levels 1 and 2 of the National Qualifications Framework.

Liz had anticipated that any issues around the management of the classroom would probably involve only occasional low-level behavioural issues of the kind that are frequently made reference to in teacher training books such as this one: students chatting to each other instead of getting on with the tasks that they had been asked to do and perhaps distracting others who are trying to work; sending text messages on their mobile phones; or asking inappropriate or perhaps embarrassing questions. But, she reasoned, behaviours such as these would be mediated or lessened by the simple fact that her AS and A2 students were attending voluntarily: they had all decided to continue their full-time education beyond the school-leaving age (although this is an issue that we shall return to later in the chapter), choosing an academic subject that may well help them progress to university, and, as such, their **intrinsic motivation** could be assumed to be high. As far as Liz was concerned, her main responsibility was to engage the extrinsic motivation of her students, through producing carefully planned lessons, stimulating – but not overly difficult – tasks and activities, and generally presenting herself as a professional, competent teacher (again, reflecting the themes and issues that she had studied during teacher training seminars and in her private reading).

Kevin, by contrast, had anticipated a very different set of behaviours from the students that he would be working with. The academy school where he was on placement was in a relatively deprived urban environment. At the school the number of students with a statement of special educational needs was higher than the national average, and the number of students achieving five 'good' GCSEs (that is, at grade C or above) was lower than the national average. Kevin expected to encounter the same low-level behaviours as Liz; but he also expected to encounter more challenging behaviours, and significant disruptions in class, reflecting the relatively low levels of intrinsic motivation that he expected to find. He was – entirely understandably – worried that he would have to manage the kinds of behaviours that might lead to a learner being excluded from a lesson. So, while Liz approached the planning, preparation and delivery of her lessons with a relatively high level of confidence and enthusiasm, Kevin's approach was rather more muted and he was rather nervous during the period leading up to his placement.

Robin's expectations were different again. He had been disappointed to learn that, during his further education college placement, he would be teaching 14- and 15-year-old students rather than 16- and 17-year-olds. Instead of teaching more highly motivated students – such as the kinds of groups Liz was expecting to be working with – he thought that he would be working with those younger students whom nobody else wanted, who had been sent to college from their secondary schools because these schools had been unable to deal with their behaviour and didn't want these students on their roll. As far as Robin was concerned, his job role would be more akin to that of a social worker than a teacher, keeping young people off the streets but not really expecting that they would engage with their courses in any meaningful sense.

Here, then, were three different trainee teachers, and three very different sets of expectations as to the kinds of behaviours that they might encounter, and why. So as the academic year progressed, how did these trainees get on?

Students' behaviours – surprises and setbacks

It's not uncommon for our teaching sessions to throw out unexpected and surprising events. Even with the most thorough lesson planning and preparation, the direction of our lessons might change. When thinking about how we manage our classrooms, our planning will always need to be accompanied by the possibility of having to think on our feet, to anticipate when things might go wrong and to close down those behaviours that might disrupt learning – something that is often learned through experience and trial-and-error as much as through formal study on a PGCE or Certificate in Education course. So what did our three trainees learn about the behaviours, motivations and aspirations of their students?

For Liz, her experiences with her AS sociology group were the cause of a significant reappraisal of her own theories and beliefs regarding students' motivation and engagement with education in the post-compulsory sector. Her assumption, that all of her students would be motivated, and hence engaged with the curriculum, turned out to be somewhat mistaken. The extent of the chatter and low-level disruption that she encountered in the seminar room was significantly greater than she had anticipated. She had gone in to the sessions expecting a bit of noise and chatter, but had found her AS group to be very noisy: phones were beeping and ringing; one learner always had her headphones on; the level of chatter was loud and some of the language used by the students was inappropriate. In this context, it is understandable that Liz found her confidence dropping. She hadn't anticipated or planned for these kinds of behaviours. Moreover, she reacted inappropriately, raising her voice and then shouting down the group. The session never really recovered after this point: planned activities were not completed or even attempted, and the subsequent session was poorly attended. Throughout, she could not really understand why students who had chosen to come to college still exhibited such disruptive behaviours.

Kevin's experiences at the academy school were also difficult for him to manage and plan for. But his story was different to Liz's story in several important ways. He had – rightly or wrongly – anticipated a high degree of low-level disruption and so he had planned accordingly. In fact, he had found that the planning process had helped him recover some of his confidence prior to the start of his placement. So when he began his placement, instead of assuming that all of his students would automatically be abiding by the academy's code of behaviour, he devoted time during his first sessions with his English and history groups to establishing ground rules for how the sessions would go. Drawing on the academy's code, he drew up a class code – in negotiation with his students – that he displayed at the front of the room. And he also took time to ask his students what they expected from him. When members of the group started to get too noisy or got distracted from the work that he had asked them to do, he kept a level head – and a level tone of voice – and reminded the group as a whole about the class code that they had all agreed. He tolerated a certain level of banter and conversation, but was quick to quietly and subtly steer his students back on track, regularly walking around the room, engaging in eye contact and eventually learning to use non-verbal gestures to keep his students focused. Working with SEN students was undoubtedly challenging for Kevin, but he was pleasantly surprised not only by how effective the provision of learning support was but also by how tolerant the rest of the students proved to be.

Robin's experiences on placement were perhaps the most surprising – and pleasant. He had gone into his placement at his further education college expecting very little from his 14- and 15-year-old students. Nonetheless he had planned a range of learning and teaching activities and a similar range of both formal and informal formative assessment tasks (later on, he admitted that much of this preparation in the first instance had been driven by the need to compile a portfolio of materials for his PGCE assignment, rather than by the need to plan for his teaching *per se*). Within a very short period of time, he found himself surprised by the extent to which his students were enjoying being at college. This is not to say that Robin did not encounter the kinds of disruptions that Liz and Kevin found. But the college environment served as a significant extrinsic motivator: Robin's students enjoyed 'not being at school' and instead being in a more grown-up environment. And although he continued to express some reservations about the Level 1 curriculum that the students were following (he was concerned that the students had unrealistic expectations about the value of the qualification in terms of future study or employability, an issue that he had researched as part of his PGCE), he found that teaching them was more enjoyable and rewarding than he had thought. Robin's engagement with the course and with his students proved to be infectious, and his enthusiasm for his teaching in turn acted as an additional extrinsic motivator.

Constructing ideas about students' behaviour

The three case studies that have been described here are important to us because they all rest on particular conceptions of learner behaviour. More specifically, they all rest on the ways in which kinds of behaviour are constructed. By this, I mean that particular assumptions, attitudes or ideas that are socially constructed govern expectations about the likely behaviour of the different groups of students with whom our three trainees were working. The notion that Liz's AS sociology students would be engaged and motivated rested on assumptions concerning the reasons why students stay in education beyond the compulsory school age, on further assumptions about their reasons for choosing that particular course, and perhaps also on stereotypical assumptions regarding the social and economic background of the group. Kevin's assumptions about the engagement and motivation of his students were similarly filtered through a series of **preconceptions**. In this case, these preconceptions revolved around the broader social and economic environment within which the academy was located – enhanced by the idea that the very fact that the school had taken on academy status was in some way a recognition that the school had previously been failing – and the educational histories of not only the students but also their parents. Finally, Robin's initial attitudes towards his students were influenced by the notion that they were in some senses all young people who had 'failed' in their compulsory schooling and as such had to have somewhere else to go – or to be sent to. The idea that a college environment might have been chosen for them because it offered the most appropriate educational provision, as distinct from a convenient way of containing the students in question, only occurred to Robin later on. In a way, their removal from mainstream schooling became conflated or confused with academic failure, lack of motivation and hence lack of engagement. Put simply, the anticipated behaviours of all of these three groups of students were taken as given, and rested on a series of assumptions about patterns of behaviours that 'would always' be exhibited by particular constituencies of students, and that were in some ways internal to those students. However, if we consider challenging or disruptive patterns of behaviour as somehow a consequence of factors that might be more or less external, not internal, to groups of students, then a very different perspective emerges.

Let me provide an example to demonstrate what can be a quite complex argument. Put simply, the idea that I am putting forward here, and which constitutes one of the key elements on which this book rests as a whole, is that in order to understand fully the very many different kinds or patterns of behaviour that we will undoubtedly encounter as teachers in the 14–19 phase, we need to see these as the consequence of a number of different phenomena that are more or less complicated. This applies whether we teach at an academy school or a further education college or anywhere else (within the current political climate, at the time of writing this book, the proliferation of different models of curriculum provision for 14–19s looks set to continue). So, for example, stating that the behaviour of students in an academy school might in some ways be a reflection of the attitudes to education and training that are held by their parents is in fact relatively uncontroversial; and, indeed, there is research to support this view. To extend this argument to students who are in a further education college studying for AS levels might seem, at first look, to be mistaken – if stereotyped views concerning the reasons why people choose to take part in education or the social and economic reasons why people choose further – and higher – education continue to be subscribed to.

If we accept stereotypical ideas such as these, then other stereotypical ideas follow: for example, that 14- to 16-year-old students who attend college courses only do so because they have failed at school, or because their school could not cope with their behaviour. In this sense, such students are effectively badged or labelled as failing, *before they have had the chance to begin their studies at their further education college*. Labelling students – or anyone else, in fact – in such a way as this can have far-reaching consequences. Take the example of Robin's college-based group. If broader societal attitudes towards students such as these are framed within discourses of failure in mainstream schooling or of challenging behaviour that schools could not cope with, then how might these impact on the students themselves – on their self-concepts? Put simply: if we spend enough time telling a learner or a group of students that they are failing, then can we be at all surprised when we find that they continue to do so, that they perceive themselves as failing within formal education and as such lose their intrinsic motivation and their academic self-concept? In this context, the break from formal schooling and the move to a further education college act as a break or marker, a moment when the students in question cross a boundary between two very different institutions and have an opportunity to reinvent themselves in a new place.

Researching the behaviour of students: 14- to 16-year-old students in further education

Harkin (2006) reported on one of the first pieces of empirical research to explore the experiences of young people aged 14–16 who were attending further education colleges, and the teaching staff who were working with them. Although this research is a few years old now – at the time of writing this chapter – it is still very useful, not least as the cross-over between school and college, and between academic and vocational curricula, is set to expand in the current political climate. Seven key themes emerged from his research:

1 Links that had already been established between schools and colleges, regarding the selection of students who might attend college, were ineffective.
2 Students felt that colleges provided an environment where they were treated 'like adults'.
3 College lecturers did not know how they should deal with any disciplinary issues that might arise.
4 Students preferred the teaching styles of college lecturers to those of their teachers at school.
5 The majority of students who came to college aged 14 needed additional support for literacy and/or numeracy.
6 Being at college instead of school led to improved attendance, improvements in behaviour and increasingly positive attitudes towards learning.
7 14–16-year-old students attending college expressed an increased interest in staying in formal education or training in the future.

Research such as this is important because it demonstrates the potential benefits of alternative provision for those young people for whom compulsory schooling is not working. Some of the issues raised are immediately understandable: the feeling of being treated 'like adults' is frequently referred to in other literature as well. Some of the issues raised need to be considered in a rather more critical manner: for example, the notion that these students would prefer the teaching styles of college lecturers rather than school teachers may be more properly rooted in a broader sense of dissatisfaction with and disengagement from school more generally, rather than be an expression of a preference for one pedagogical approach over another. And some of the issues raised are troublesome: the numbers of young people who come into further education college – and this might be adult students or 16-year-olds as well as 14-year-olds – who need additional support for either numeracy and/or literacy, is too high. Why have these needs not been picked up or acted upon before now?

Researching the behaviour of students: students' perceptions of indiscipline and exclusion

McCluskey's (2008) account of her research in four secondary schools in Scotland provides findings that are, in a manner similar to those of Harkin (2006), at odds with popular or stereotypical conceptions of students' behaviour. Her research focused on the perceptions and attitudes of students, as opposed to parents, carers or professionals. She found a high level of consensus among students, whether they attended schools with high exclusion rates or low exclusion rates, concerning three key issues:

1 Exclusion was largely seen as a form of punishment, but not one that would have any subsequent impact on learner behaviour or attitude.

2 Schools' and teachers' responses to disruptive patterns of behaviour at school were largely seen as ineffective; students reported that blame was often apportioned according to reputation, and that teachers were inconsistent in their approach.

3 Low levels of disruptive behaviour (such as shouting out, forgetting homework or interrupting the teacher) were exhibited by a majority of students from time to time, of whom only a minority would be classified as coming from 'difficult' or 'complex' backgrounds.

What are we to make of the findings of this research? Admittedly, this research draws on a small-scale case study of just four schools, but the findings are nonetheless significant. It would appear to be the case that *students* perceive exclusion to have no meaningful impact on behaviour: and yet many parents, government ministers and schools argue the opposite and position exclusion (of varying forms) as part of their broader approach to behaviour management. Patterns of low-level disruptive behaviour appear to be quite widely distributed among the student population, but it is invariably those with a reputation for troublemaking who receive sanctions: a paradigmatic example of the kinds of inconsistent teacher behaviour that the students in this study commented on.

Labelling students

Beginning to unpack why particular attitudes regarding some groups of students – or, indeed, attitudes about any particular social, economic or cultural groups – persist is a complicated and politically charged activity. Nor is this process of unpacking made easier by the 'moral outrage' of tabloid newspapers or broadcasters who complain that discipline in schools is in a perilous state. **Labelling theory**, a concept drawn from sociology, offers us a useful way to consider how it is that some people or groups of people are labelled as 'deviating' from the established norms or rules of society or some element of social behaviour (whatever these might mean – an issue to which I shall return and which is explored further in Chapter 3).

Let us return to Robin's group of students aged 14–16. These young people had been successfully labelled in all kinds of ways: as failing in compulsory formal schooling; as being troublesome; as performing below national benchmarks for educational attainment by age 16. But in order for such labels or descriptions to stick, they need to be attributed to the young people in question by other people who are sufficiently influential or powerful to persuade society at large that such labels are justified and appropriate. If a group of people are going to be labelled as having broken some rules (in this case, rules about behaviour, educational progress and certified achievement in examinations), then we need also to remember that the labelling process requires people to make these rules in the first place, and then other people to enforce them. Before he met his students, Robin had already begun to make certain assumptions about them: about how they would behave, and the extent to which they would be motivated – or not – to learn. Robin's perceptions of these students had been informed in a number of related ways. The 'norm' is that young people stay at school until 16 and take GCSEs (or other equivalent qualifications – however, at the time of writing this chapter, the Education Secretary, Michael Gove, has announced that many of the vocational awards that had been given 'equivalency' to GCSEs are in future no longer going to contribute to school league tables). Other norms relate to how young people in schools – or colleges – are expected to behave.

Now, all of these attitudes, perspectives – call them what you will – are socially constructed and socially mediated. That is to say, there is no 'absolute' or 'definitive' definition of what constitutes good behaviour: the model of good behaviour that young people are expected to subscribe to is a social creation, made up of people's attitudes, expectations, stereotypes and opinions. It is simply the case that some people in society are more influential than others in setting the rules that members of that society at large are expected to follow. However, just as these rules are socially constructed, so are opinions about these very kinds of groups of students who are seen as being troublesome. There is nothing 'automatically' disruptive about particular kinds of behaviour of young people in schools or colleges. It only becomes disruptive when powerful people – schoolteachers, college lecturers, governors and ministers – say that it is. But the problem here, as evidenced by not only McCluskey's (2008) research but other research as well, is that these ascriptions of disruptive behaviour are similarly socially constructed. And this is why they are inconsistent: because people will, quite simply, assume that some kinds of students are more likely than others to misbehave, or to be more likely to 'fail' in academic terms, or similar. And it is important to note that assumptions such as these can cause preconceptions of all kinds. Robin drew on what might be termed a deficit model regarding his students: he assumed that they lacked particular motivations, attitudes and behaviours. Liz, by contrast, when beginning to teach her AS sociology group for the first time, assumed that her students would all possess those very characteristics – but this turned out not to be the case. A group of students whom she thought would be articulate, motivated and keen to make progress in fact possessed a much more spiky profile: so how can we make sense not only of Liz's preconceptions, but the quite different reality that presented itself to her when she began her teaching placement?

Liz's assumptions about her AS sociology group rest on labelling to the same extent as Robin's assumptions about his students. If students are over 16, free to choose which subjects they should study at AS/A2 (or any other NQF Level 3 curriculum offered in a sixth form or further education college), then surely they should be highly motivated to learn? Surely the kinds of external factors that might impact on the behaviour of other students (such as the groups that Robin and Kevin were teaching) would not apply here? In fact, if Liz – or anyone else who was working with students in a further education or sixth form college – were to ask longer-standing members of staff about motivation, engagement and attitude among the students, the answer would be quite different. Just as Robin's 14–16 group have been labelled as a problem group, so Liz's 16–18 group have been labelled as well: as having chosen to stay on in full-time education for unproblematic or uncomplicated reasons: to help them get a better job at the end of their course, or to gain the qualifications that they need to go to university. Their intrinsic motivation is assumed to be at a high level. But these assumptions need to be unpacked. What if sociology was a second choice, the result of having done less well at GCSE level than hoped for? What if the decision to stay in education had been made in the light of parental pressure, or peer pressure (if all of your friends were going to college, would you not want to stay on as well?)? Simply put, it is not necessarily the case that students in post-compulsory education have straightforwardly 'chosen' to stay on in college. How might such a group be composed two years from now, when education until the age of 18 becomes compulsory?

The importance of inclusion

At the beginning of this chapter, I posed the question: 'Why should we include all students?' Now, having considered some of the complexities that surround learner behaviour, motivation and engagement – positive manifestations of which are necessary prerequisites for successful learning – we can return to the broader issue of inclusive practice in education.

Inclusion is a broad term, which encompasses students, staff, the curriculum – in fact, all areas of educational provision:

- Valuing all students and staff equally.
- Increasing the participation of students in, and reducing their exclusion from, the cultures, curricula and communities of local schools.
- Restructuring the cultures, policies and practices in schools so that they respond to the diversity of students in the locality.
- Reducing barriers to learning and participation for all students, not only those with impairments or those who are categorized as 'having special educational needs'.
- Learning from attempts to overcome barriers to the access and participation of particular students to make changes for the benefit of students more widely.
- Viewing the difference between students as resources to support learning, rather than as problems to be overcome.
- Acknowledging the right of students to an education in their locality.
- Improving schools for staff as well as for students.
- Emphasizing the role of schools in building community and developing values, as well as in increasing achievement.
- Fostering mutually sustaining relationships between schools and communities.
- Recognizing that inclusion in education is one aspect of inclusion in society.

(CSIE 2012)

A definition such as this, which includes but also transcends issues such as whether or not someone has a learning difficulty or disability (as understood in the 2010 Equality Act), positions inclusion as something more than simply a series of techniques or even philosophies that facilitate the acquisition of an academic, technical or vocational curriculum by the broadest possible constituency of students. It foregrounds the broader social role that education can and must occupy.

But there is a difficult tension here that still needs to be resolved. An inclusive approach such as this is entirely laudable. And yet at the same time we have to acknowledge that there are some students aged between 14 and 19 who – for all kinds of reasons – do not like being in formal education or training. Now, current plans by the coalition government to raise the school-leaving age to 18 (within three years from the time of writing this chapter) are not so crude as to assume that what counts as 'school' means just that: other forms of provision – in further education colleges, in employment, following technical and vocational programmes in the workplace – will also be permissible. Greater alignment between providers of training and employers would appear to be particularly significant, not least as research increasingly demonstrates that an engagement with the world of work is a highly effective way of encouraging young people to stay in formal education or training and prevent them from drifting into being NEET (Mann et al. 2010).

Wanting to include all students through an inclusive agenda is not the same thing as making everyone be students as a consequence of raising the age at which a young person can choose to leave education or training voluntarily. At some point, we need to consider the extent to which it is appropriate to make the assumption that all young people, up to and including age 18, should be in formal education or training: if a young person does not want to be in education or training, does he or she not have the right to say so? How might the kinds of complex behaviours that Liz, Kevin and Robin encountered be compounded if even more people were 'made' to stay in education or training? If people are able to and want to find employment instead, should that not be allowed? There are ways in which this could be accomplished: the workplace as a place of learning is well researched and the benefits of learning on the job, and of having that learning formally accredited, do not need to be rehearsed here (Malloch et al. 2011). But vocational and technical education and training remain underfunded and undervalued in relation to the academic curriculum: a form of provision for 'other people's children'. Unless this attitude can be changed, educational inequalities will persist. And as long as some forms of education and training are seen as being second best, then can it be any wonder that, whatever the age of the learner, there is resistance to participation and hence to learning?

Recommended reading

Leathwood, C. (2006) Gendered constructions of lifelong learning and the learner in the UK policy context, in C. Leathwood and B. Francis (eds) *Gender and Lifelong Learning: Critical Feminist Engagements*. London: Routledge.

Mittler, P. (2000) *Working Towards Inclusive Education: Social Contexts*. London: David Fulton.

Thomas, G. and Vaughan, M. (2004) *Inclusive Education: Readings and Reflections*. Maidenhead: Open University Press.

References

CSIE (Centre for Studies in Inclusive Education) (2012) Website available at: http://www.csie.org.uk/.

Harkin, J. (2006) Treated like adults: 14–16-year-olds in further education, *Research in Post-Compulsory Education*, 11(3): 319–39.

Malloch, M., Cairns, L., Evans, K. and O'Connor, B. (eds) (2011) *The Sage Handbook of Workplace Learning*. London: Sage Publications.

Mann, A., Lopez, D. and Stanley, J. (2010) *What Is to Be Gained Through Partnerships? Exploring the Value of Education–Employer Relationships*. London: Education and Employers Taskforce.

McCluskey, M. (2008) Exclusion from school: what can 'included' pupils tell us?, *British Educational Research Association*, 34(4): 447–66.

CHAPTER

3

An exploration of why students behave in the way they do

By the end of this chapter, you will be able to:

- critically explore why students behave the way they do;
- apply a range of sociological and psychological concepts to behaviour awareness and management;
- demonstrate an awareness of the impact of labelling on teacher and learner behaviour and attitudes;
- understand the medical and social models of special educational needs and disability, with a focus on ADHD.

Introduction: the *why* of behaviour

There are all kinds of theories explaining students' behaviour, not just misbehaviour that interferes with teaching and with students' learning but other behaviours that make it difficult for students to do as well as they might do. For reflective practitioners (see Chapter 6), trying to understand why students behave the way they do can sometimes prove difficult. Even when we take the time to reflect on the actions of others, sometimes we just cannot figure out why some students react one way and other students react in a completely opposite way. This can be particularly puzzling when we are using the same teaching and learning strategies but the outcomes are very different in terms of motivation and engagement. When we are faced with challenging student behaviour, reaction time is often instantaneous to things that we see and experience. However, when the process is broken down, we can start to unpick and understand what and why certain behaviour is happening. When we observe the behaviour, it is important to consider the lens we are looking through. This will be strongly influenced by the flow of our values, assumptions, beliefs and expectations (ABE) that have been and continue to be shaped by our own life journey and experiences. It is through the flow of ABE that we form our perceptions and then our judgements of the behaviour event we have observed. Subsequently this leads us to an assumption about what we have just experienced. Once we have reached our deduction our immediate feelings and emotions come into play and lead us to react to the behaviour in a particular way. A starting point to understanding our students' behaviour is to understand ourselves; we must recognize and understand the causes of our behaviours.

Activity 3.1

Consider the following:

- How do you manage your class and why?
- What teaching and learning strategies do you implement in your classroom to promote active engagement and why?
- How do you react to challenging behaviour and why?
- Read the narrative below and consider your own classroom management organization.

A teacher's classroom management organization communicates information about the teacher's beliefs on content and the learning process. It also illustrates the types of instruction that will take place in a particular classroom. For example, a classroom in which the teacher takes complete responsibility for guiding students' actions constitutes a different learning environment than one in which students are encouraged and taught to assume responsibility for their own behaviours. Content will be approached and understood differently in each of these settings.

Labelling and stigma

Practitioners can play a large role in undermining students' function-ing, specifically through labelling. Labelling students can have an im-pact on learning and, importantly, on their confidence and self-esteem. **Labelling theory**, although initially applied to sociological studies of deviant behaviour by Howard Becker in the 1950s and 1960s, has been widely researched in the field of education in order to determine stu-dents' academic outcomes based on the labels they have been given in class and, subsequently, the expectations of the teachers within their schools and colleges. Becker argues that it is not the individuals' actions but the social reaction to those actions that creates deviance. His ideas are important as they can highlight how those in a position of power (such as classroom practitioners) can label individuals as deviant. This can lead to practitioner's lowered expectations, as well as more negative stereotypes and attitudes towards the labelled.

Labelling in the classroom is like other types of stereotyping – it is an unconscious process and consequently done automatically. The worthy intentions that were the catalyst for many practitioners going into teaching

❛❛ 'to help students' achieve their potential and lead rich and
fruitful lives'   ❜❜

can be quickly undermined when these practitioners begin to treat their students differently based on their academic achievement, or other factors which shape the students' identity such as class, gender and ethnicity. These practitioners can find it extremely difficult to acknowledge the discrepancy between their cognitions of wanting to create an equal classroom and their actions of creating inequality.

The more awareness practitioners have on how detrimental this unintentional action can be for their students, the better prepared teachers will be in recognizing the bias they enact with their students, preventing socially disadvantaged students or those experiencing other structural inequalities from internalizing this label and allowing it to dictate their potential as both a student and as an individual.

Erving Goffman (1959), whose work focuses on the analysis of every-day interactions, compared social life to the theatre and as such his perspective of the self is dramaturgical, much like a performance. Dependent on the context, different roles are acted out. The roles we can choose from are based on patterns of behaviour, responses and routines, like parts in a play. Goffman offers a frame to explore the links between the society in which the students live and the limitations offered by the roles they play. Goffman's (1963) work on stigma facilitates the exploration of the relationship between the students' interactions, individual attributes and labelling. Stigma is socially situated and may occur when an individual is identified as deviant and linked with negative stereotypes, such as being labelled 'thick' and/or 'poor'. This can engender prejudiced attitudes, which can lead to discriminatory behaviour towards the person. In turn, this can impact on the person experiencing low self-esteem. The stigma process is dependent on the social, economic and political power necessary to impose discriminatory experiences on the labelled individual or group. Advantaged groups can stigmatize less advantaged groups, such as the poor, to justify why they have more. According to Goffman, stigma can be classed under three categories:

1 tribal identities;
2 abominations of the body; and
3 blemish of individual character (Goffman 1963: 4).

These are not mutually exclusive. In research carried out by Vicky Duckworth which followed the learning journey of sixteen basic skills students, she identified the impact on learning of being labelled (Duckworth 2011). Stella, in the research group, opened up about how the teachers at junior school labelled her and the other 'scruffy' kids who struggled with their school work:

> 66 The teacher tied me left hand to a chair and tried to get me to write with me right hand... I went home heartbroken... [From then on, she would go in to school for her mark and then 'wag it'.] The teachers didn't care about us scruffy kids . . . kids from poor families were left to do whatever they liked.
>
> (Duckworth 2011) 99

Here we see how Stella clearly identifies how, as a member of the working class and being poor, her tribal identity was seen as a blemish on her individual character. Indeed, Steedman (1988) identifies how children are labelled as early as primary school. The semi-skilled and unskilled working class that she and her colleagues taught was not 'how children ought to be, not "real" children' – though they represented most of the children in society. She points out the urgency to 'outline the history that has made working class childhood into a kind of pathology in this way' (Steedman 1988: 82). It is this very pathology which Vicky addressed when seeking to explore schooling as a site of institutionalized capital (see Reay 2005, Duckworth and Cochrane 2012, Thomas et al. 2012), where people define themselves and their social worth (Luttrell 1997).

Activity 3.2

Consider the following:

- The expectations/aspirations you have for your students and why.

You may want to consider how this is shaped by your own beliefs, values and assumptions on what makes a *good* and *poor* student. I use these words deliberately as a lever to help unpick bias around notions of 'successful' and 'unsuccessful' students.

Teachers' expectation

Clearly the way practitioners view learners and the labels they hang on them (good/bad) bring expectations (achiever/non-achiever) which inevitably affect the way they interact with them, and ultimately lead to changes in students' behaviour and attitude. Let us explore this in a little more detail. In a classic study performed by Robert Rosenthal, elementary school teachers were given IQ scores for all of their students, scores that did not reflect IQ and, in reality, measured nothing. Yet, just as researchers expected, teachers formed a positive expectation for those students who scored high on the exam as opposed to those who scored low. We can see here how labelling theory can be linked to teacher expectation and self-fulfilling prophesy (see Ball 1981). Activities by the practitioner leading to students being labelled as 'intelligent', 'slow', 'average' can sometimes result from negative attitudes and labelling due to fear and a lack of awareness about the particular needs of students or the potential barriers which they may face.

The key to a supportive classroom environment is a practitioner who is willing to challenge negative labels and in doing so establish a caring relationship with each student, learn about a student's individual needs and strengths, and offer the support and encouragement each student needs to reach his or her potential. Students with behavioural issues will benefit from practitioners who are committed to an inclusive classroom, organized, plan for potential challenges and establish secure classrooms where students feel valued. Part of feeling valued includes practitioners recognizing and addressing the barriers to learning which students face and how this impacts on behaviour and motivation.

Activity 3.3

Consider the following:

- The barriers to learning that students face.

You may want to consider:

- individual differences;
- differences in family patterns;
- learning difficulty/disability;
- environmental factors;
- psychological factors.

Barriers to learning

Negative and damaging attitudes towards difference in society remain a critical barrier to learning and development. Discriminatory approaches resulting from prejudice against people on the basis of race, class, gender, culture, disability, religion, ability, sexual preference and other characteristics manifest themselves as barriers to learning when such attitudes are focused towards students in the education system.

Poverty and attainment

Although the relationship between poverty and attainment is well researched, there is less clear understanding of strategies which address this and offer interventions and strategies for raising attainment for children and young people from disadvantaged backgrounds. We must remember that students behave inappropriately for a reason. As practitioners we should seek to find the reasons why. The questions we may ask include:

- What does the student aim to gain from their behaviour?
- Is the student tired, hungry, bored, worried, angry, sad, etc.?

Home environments

'Environment' can be defined as a student's home shared with parents, spouses, extended family carers or friends, or outside in the neighbourhood and community. In Maslow's hierarchy of needs, environmental factors are towards the top of the pyramid. Needless to say, the environments which students experience have an impact on their learning, behaviour and attitude. For example, a child who comes from a violent neighbourhood may be more likely to participate in negative activities, such as gangs and fighting. Counter to this, a positive neighbourhood environment may promote students' social, mental and physical development. The neighbourhood environment can also impact on whether students feel safe or in danger on the streets in which they live.

An environment of poverty can have an impact on students' experience of education. For example, students living in low-income households may not have the opportunity because their parents/carers/they are unable to meet the costs of pastoral activities, trips, after-school clubs, resources such as books, a computer, and so on. Reay et al. (2005: 19) highlight how school success is linked by 'the amount and type of cultural capital inherited from the family milieu rather than by measures of individual talent or achievement'.

Joseph Rowntree's report, *The Importance of Attitudes and Behaviour for Poorer Children's Educational Attainment*, highlights the impact of an environment of poverty on students' experience of education (Goodman and Gregg 2010)

- The aspirations, attitudes and behaviour of parents and children potentially play an important part in explaining why poor children typically do worse at school.
- Children from poorer backgrounds are much less likely to experience a rich home learning environment than children from better-off backgrounds. At age 3, reading to the child and the wider home learning environment are very important for children's educational development.
- The gap between children from richer and poorer backgrounds widens especially quickly during primary school. Some of the factors that appear to explain this are:
  - parental aspirations for higher education;
  - how far parents and children believe their own actions can affect their lives; and children's behavioural problems.
- It becomes harder to reverse patterns of under-achievement by the teenage years, but disadvantage and poor school results continue to be linked, including through teenagers' and parents' expectations for higher education.
- Material resources such as access to a computer and the internet at home; engagement in anti-social behaviour; and young people's belief in their own ability at school.

The report findings clearly illustrate the impact of environment and poverty in shaping students' experience of education and their life chances.

The study also notes that young people are more likely to do well at GCSE if *the young person* him/herself:

66
- has a greater belief in his/her own ability at school;
- believes that events result primarily from his/her own behaviour and actions;
- finds school worthwhile;

- thinks it is likely that he/she will apply to, and get into, higher education;
- avoids risky behaviour such as frequent smoking, cannabis use, anti-social behaviour, truancy, suspension and exclusion; and
- does not experience bullying.

(Goodman and Gregg 2010) 🙾

So how can we as practitioners intervene and provide a learning environment which challenges the injustices of social and economic deprivation and provides opportunities for *all* students to flourish, irrespective of their background? As a starting point, by getting to know the student you can start to build a relationship based on trust and respect.

Abraham Maslow, in his book *Motivation and Personality* (1954), suggests that people are motivated by their individual needs to address certain natural concerns. These concerns, in turn, can be ranked hierarchically in terms of importance. He consequently proposed a five-level hierarchy of needs:

1 physiological needs;
2 safety needs;
3 belongingness needs;
4 esteem needs; and
5 self-actualization needs.

Physiological needs are the most basic human needs such as hunger, thirst, and shelter. Safety needs refer to the desire to find a safe and secure physical environment. Belongingness needs allude to an individual's desire to be accepted by his or her peers, while esteem needs refer to the desire to have a positive self-image and to receive recognition from others. **Self-actualization** needs are at the top of the pyramid and represent the concern for the development of full individual potential. You may want to draw on a humanistic view of education, to develop and implement strategies to address the barriers to learning your students face.

Activity 3.4

Consider the following:

- Which factors do you consider create a positive learning environment?
- Is the space warm and inviting?
- Does the room arrangement match your philosophy of learning?
- Do the students have access to necessary resources?
- Are the distracting features of a room eliminated?

Remember:

Creating and implementing a learning environment means careful planning for the start of the academic year. The learning environment must be envisioned as both a physical space and a cognitive space. The physical space of the classroom is managed as the teacher prepares the classroom for the students. Attending to these and similar questions aids a teacher in managing the physical space of the classroom and addressing Maslow's hierarchy of needs.

Motivation

Motivation is a key driver in stimulating students and providing an educational experience which offers them the opportunity to be productive and have self-respect. It can challenge the inequalities in the learners' lives and provide them with hope and aspirations, which challenge the cycle of poverty and failure.

In any area where we intend to inspire motivation, setting both short-term and long-range goals is needed. If the long-term goals clearly contribute to the students' aims in life, they should be more motivating.

The reflective case study below explores goal setting and motivation.

Case study: Louise Losztyn

Louise is a PGCE student in Post Compulsory Education and Training (PCET) and a specialist in dance and drama.

Reflecting on a lesson with a focus on Target Setting

This journal entry was written after teaching 'Devising' to a BTEC First (Level 2) Diploma in Drama and Dance. I have chosen to write this reflection based on a combination of Kolb's Learning Cycle (Kolb 1984) and Rolfe's Framework for Reflective Practice ('What?' 'So what?' and 'Now what?') (Rolfe et al. (2001), as I feel they are both suited to this specific reflection and fit together well.

What?

I filmed the students performing their devised group pieces in order for them to engage in self-assessment and set themselves developmental targets for improvement. Wlodkowski (2008) suggests that engaging adult students in self-assessment processes can exceedingly increase their competency within their subject area.

I have 7 female students and 1 male learner in the group, and as the male learner handed me back his feedback form I noticed that he had ticked '1' (outstanding) in every area of critique. I challenged him on this and he stated 'I thought my performance was perfect, I think I did better than everyone else so I don't really think I need a target.'

Gardner et al. (2000) believe that individual target setting rather than group target setting enables a focus on each individual student's varied needs and abilities, rather than over-challenging some students and patronizing others. They also believe that there is always room for improvement within an individual's academia, which is something I strongly believe in, especially within the performing arts.

Due to my supported belief, I sat with the learner and employed the use of subsidiary questions until he realized that this was actually a positive activity focused on self-improvement for increased achievement, rather than merely useless self-critique.

So what?

Initially when the learner alleged he was 'the best', I felt like informing him that in actual fact there were many areas where he needed drastic improvement to occur, if he was going to even scrape a pass. However, I refrained from doing this and took his remark as an opportunity to understand why the learner may have felt like this, rather than immediately judging him, which was something I found difficult to avoid when I first began teaching.

I concluded in my mind that possibly he may have felt inferior to the rest of the group as he was the only male learner, and therefore desired to maintain the alpha male role by reassuring himself that he was better at his performance than all of the females. Reynolds and Miller (2003) discuss how various psychological experiments have demonstrated that in education males yearn to avoid being outsmarted by their female peers, in order to evade unwanted peer pressure and a diminishment of their masculinity.

Now what?

This experience introduced a strategy to me that I hadn't thought about before: in the future when I am engaging my students in self/peer assessment exercises, I will title the feedback hand-outs more positively, for example 'Targets for improvement' rather than 'Constructive criticism'. Barnes (1999) believes that optimistic teaching results in optimistic learning which, overall, leads to bright and positive academic success.

This occurrence also reinforced the reality of teaching performing arts, which is that some students are more confident than others. It reminded me that as the teacher it is my job not only to stretch the more confident students, but also to implement strategies in order to boost the self-esteem of my less confident students, for example by engaging them in group work with their peers.

Attribution theory and motivation

A theory that can help us to further understand behaviour and motivation is attribution theory. Heider (1958) was the first to propose a psychological theory of attribution. In Heider's view, people were like amateur scientists, trying to understand other people's behaviour by piecing together information until they arrived at a rational explanation or cause. Attribution theory is concerned with *how* and *why* people explain events as they do. So it makes sense that the better we know someone, the more likely we are to attribute behaviour to the situation. According to Heider, a person can make two attributions:

Internal attribution: the suggestion that a person is behaving in a certain way because of something about the person, such as attitude, character or personality.

External attribution: the suggestion that a person is behaving in a certain way because of something about the situation she or he is in.

So let us consider how we can draw on attribution theory in the educational context. Attribution theory has been used to explain the difference in motivation between high and low achievers. According to attribution theory, high achievers will approach rather than avoid tasks related to succeeding, because they believe success is due to high ability and effort, in which they are confident. Failure is understood to be caused by bad luck or a bad assignment (not their fault). Thus, failure does not lower their self-esteem but success builds pride and confidence. They tend to persist when the work gets hard rather than giving up because failure is supposed to be caused by a lack of effort, which they can alter by trying harder. They also tend to work with a lot of energy because the results are believed to be determined by how hard they try and the effort they put into the task. Conversely, low achievers avoid success-related tasks because they tend to doubt their ability and/or consider that success is related to luck or to other influences outside their grasp, and so beyond their control. Consequently, even when successful, it is not as gratifying to the low achiever because they do not feel responsible; it does not increase their self-confidence and belief in their abilities.

Case study: Michael Lowey

Michael is a PGCE PCET student specializing in photography and is based at Skelmersdale College in the North-West of England in the town of Skelmersdale.

Skelmersdale: a portrait and a 50th year celebration

As part of a regional 50th birthday celebration for a particular 'New Town' and the opening of a new £43 million campus at the local Grade 1

Outstanding (Ofsted) college in the North-West of England, a number of AS, A2, NCFE (Level 1) and NCFE (Level 2) photography students were required to undertake a number of photography workshops (each lasting two hours) concerned with the documentation of the town in question. The images would be assessed and those considered 'worthy' would be exhibited, first, within the new college building and then in an exhibition at a local gallery. The 'winning' photographer (best image) would be offered a personal exhibition within the gallery in question.

Originally, the workshop had been publicized as being open to the public; however, after little interest, the students were required to attend in order to make up the required numbers (for financial reasons). Although the assessed work was not relevant to their particular qualification, those attending were selected for a variety of reasons including being high achievers, displaying low motivation, having poor attendance, requiring additional teaching input and having shown a genuine interest in attending. The town in question (and its inhabitants) have received much negative publicity over a period of many years, with poor-quality housing, crime rates, unemployment figures, broken families, teenage pregnancies and drug and alcohol issues rising rapidly. As such, many of the students have been excluded from compulsory education due to the barriers they have faced and have extremely low self-esteem, considering their chances of success to be very low given their surroundings and the many local examples of educational and economic failure.

My experience

As I wanted to motivate and re-engage the students I put a number of strategies into place to promote their enthusiasm for photography and challenge the negative experiences that they initially brought into the classroom. I asked the students to bring a number of images of the local area with them (taken by themselves) to be reviewed, in order that suggestions for improvement or alternative viewpoints could be made. In the case of images considered to be appropriate, assistance with editing (software) could be offered.

However, most students did *not* arrive at the session with images. Since the session was relatively short (two hours) and students had to remain in location (for health and safety reasons), the plan was for the content to include classroom-based activities, such as group critique of sample images, viewing of video and slideshows and practical experience with editing software (Photoshop). The sample images used during the session were appropriate to all age groups and also appropriate to the town in question in terms of style and content. I checked with all students that the room was adequately warm and/or ventilated. I laid the room out in a 'horseshoe' shape so that all students could see the front and each other. All of the students had access to a computer with the relevant software at their seating position. All students were also provided with a 'digital' handout (Microsoft Word) available on their own college storage space, complete with sample images. They were instructed as to the location of the document and advised how the font size, background or text colour could be amended. The handout provided a step-by-step 'how to' guide to all aspects of the session including the various tools available in the editing software. I purposefully made reference to the reputation of the town within their delivery and challenged the students to produce images that showed the town in a more truthful manner, while not hiding from the negative aspects that could also be recorded. The students were encouraged to draw upon their own experiences to create a true and balanced documentation of their town.

Factors considered as potential barriers to learning prior to the session included:

- home environments and/or circumstances;
- motivation;
- attribution theory – students' own self-perception will often influence their motivation, involvement and interpretation of the success or failure of their current efforts and hence their future likelihood to achieve.
  - Crucially, the students are likely to attribute their successes or failures to factors that will enable them to feel as good as possible about themselves. In general, this means that when students succeed at a task, they are likely to want to attribute this success to their own efforts or abilities; but when they fail, they will want to attribute their failure to factors over which they have no control, such as environment.
  - In general terms, attribution theory implies that the students' own self-perception of success and failure determines the volume and quality of effort they will make in completing an activity.

Impact of a lack of motivation on a low achiever

Teaching the lower achievers can be very challenging. Students can switch off completely, or use a range of disruptive tactics to cover their lack of confidence. When students underachieve, their capacity and skills find no expression. This can result in them becoming disaffected, and they may well disrupt others in the class. As we struggle to manage their challenging behaviour, our job satisfaction can diminish and in turn the morale of the class can suffer. Underachieving students create a real challenge for practitioners, but it is a *challenge* that needs addressing. Resolving underachievement can support practitioners to develop their teaching and learning strategies. This can make teaching rewarding and emotionally fulfilling.

> **Activity 3.5**
> Consider how you might motivate a low achiever.

Strategies to motivate students

It is important that as practitioners we work towards providing a learning environment where learning is valued. If students believe in the importance of the task you set, this can improve achievement and motivation. Measures can be taken to shift attributions of the low achievers from external factors to internal factors, so that they may become enthusiastic and motivated students. These internal factors can be related to the students' long- and short-term goals, for example their career aspirations, hobbies, personal hopes for the future. When students are motivated to learn, they are more likely to persist even when challenged.

- Establish why your students are not motivated. There are different reasons why students may lack motivation, such as having low self-esteem, difficulties at home, a learning disability, health issues and/or depression.
- Demonstrate enthusiasm and energy in the classroom. This can really motivate and engage students. Don't hold back from showing

emotions of excitement about the topics you are teaching and activities you are using. This will help hold the students' attention and actively promote their interest in learning.

- Actively encourage your students to participate in class. While some students will enjoy participating in class activities/ discussions, others may be cautious about the attention this brings. However, in an inclusive classroom it is vital that all students have an opportunity to participate in your lessons. You may want to differentiate Questioning and Answering techniques, such as open, closed, direct, scaffolded, and apply Bloom's critical thinking questioning strategies to encourage a wide variety of feedback.
- Use positive feedback in the classroom.
- Learning to learn: teaching your students techniques and strategies to enable them to research topics, study at home, use the internet and library to access key information.
- Know their strengths and weaknesses and how to set realistic yet challenging goals. Offer students the opportunity to reflect on their progress, which makes explicit the knowledge/skills gained.
- Ensure that the task will give all students experiences of succeeding to develop their self-esteem.

Managing the group and motivation

As a practitioner, understanding about the internal dynamics of the group and how to manage different students will make group working more effective. There are some common problems with communications which can be helped by active facilitation by the practitioner.

The persistent talker

This student monopolizes group discussions.

Strategy

- summarize their main points and divert the discussion to others;
- interrupt with a yes/no question and ask someone else to comment;

- give them a specific task (e.g. note taking, writing on a flipchart/white/smart board) so that they have to listen to others;
- divide class into groups for specific tasks.

Always tries to answer every question first

Strategy

- recognize their help;
- seek out several answers to include other members of the class;
- use direct questioning to other students;
- encourage members of the class to ask questions.

Talking to others nearby and not joining in with the whole group

Strategy

- address them directly and ask them to contribute to the whole group;
- stop talking until they realize others are listening.

The quiet student

This student may be shy and timid, speaking quietly or cannot find the words to say what he or she means.

Strategy

- support them by allowing time for them to respond and not feeling under pressure to answer questions immediately;
- initially ask questions they are able to answer, such as basic questions;
- protect them from mockery or teasing by providing a safe environment based on students respecting each other and what they each have to say;
- acknowledge their contribution;
- put the group into pairs on a task to increase confidence.

Negative attitude

These students may like to communicate in class but have a negative attitude that can have an impact and affect others. They may act superior as though they have nothing to learn and indeed know everything.

Strategy

- ask for specific examples of issues they raise;
- ask the group to comment;
- then ask the person to summarize the rest of the group's points;
- indicate to the group that they will learn more if everyone shares experience and knowledge.

The complainer

This student blames others and frequently finds fault.

Strategy

- encourage them to be specific about the problem and invite the group to think of positive solutions;
- be direct and say that the group has to get on with the task.

The arguer

This student may be aggressive on a regular basis, hostile and antagonistic.

Strategies

- acknowledge that they feel strongly about the issue and invite comments from the group;
- avoid lengthy debates by saying you can discuss this after the session;
- defuse the situation and then continue with the class;
- as a final option, ask them to leave the class group.

Attachment theory

To gain a greater understanding into the relationship between the teacher and student and the impact of this on learning and behaviour management, it is worth exploring attachment theory. This theory is concerned with the relationships between people (teacher and students). Bowlby (1969) asserts that attachment theory explains how students use their positive relationships with adults to organize their experiences. Central to this theory is that students with close relationships with their teachers view their teacher as a 'secure base' from which to explore the classroom environment. In practice, students with this 'secure base' feel safe when making mistakes and feel more relaxed, accepting the academic trials necessary for learning.

How practitioners form and maintain classroom relationships is crucial to the success of their work. A practitioner who is able to accurately interpret the underlying relationship processes can learn to influence the dynamics of any class proactively, rather than reactively. Fostering positive, attentive interactions with students that build secure attachments requires knowledge and experience. This can subsequently influence their confidence and self-esteem as they move into adulthood. Positive attachments can lead to students displaying:

- a willingness to explore;
- a positive view of themselves;
- an understanding of empathy;
- an ability to express emotions.

Indeed, students whose diminished self-esteem and resilience are limitations on engagement in relationships and emotional and cognitive development can struggle to reach their potential both in and out of the classroom. The reasons for this are varied and complex and their difficulties can be compounded by the responses they elicit in others. By building positive attachments with students, the more vulnerable, who have perhaps previously had negative experiences of education, can begin to re-experience more positive and hopeful relationships and greater emotional well-being, and engage more successfully in learning. Successful engagement in education and learning is the access point to later engagement in the social world of work and their communities.

Activity 3.6

Consider the strategies you can put in place to establish a positive learning environment:

- Increase your knowledge and experience of interacting with students.
- Know and demonstrate knowledge about individual students' backgrounds, interests, emotional strengths and academic levels.
- Express warm, positive and enthusiastic responses as you interact with students.
- Be attentive to your students' learning needs.
- Show your pleasure and enjoyment of students.
- Interact in a responsive and respectful manner.

If a student feels a personal connection to a teacher, experiences frequent communication with a teacher, and receives more guidance and praise than criticism from the teacher, then the student is likely to become more trustful of that teacher, show more engagement in the academic content presented, display better classroom behaviour, and achieve at higher levels academically. Positive teacher–student relationships draw students into the process of learning and promote their desire to learn (given that the content material of the class is engaging, promotes anti-discriminatory practice and is age-appropriate).

Effective dialogue

Ensure that you are mindful of what you say to the challenging students in your classroom. Are you constantly barraging them with requests to do something or telling them to stop doing what they are doing? No one likes being persistently pestered, and your students are no exception. Instead, you should find a time or place when you can have a positive discussion with the challenging student. Perhaps this could be in a tutorial.

Are you giving students meaningful feedback that says you care about them and their learning, or are you in a rush to cram this in? In your conversations, are you focusing on what your students have accomplished or are you concentrating your comments on what they have not yet grasped? Do your body positions, facial expressions and tone/intonation of voice show your students that you are interested in them? Are you telling them to do one thing, yet modelling quite different behaviour? For example, are you telling your students to be respectful to each other, but then raising your voice and demeaning students in class? Be sure that the feedback you give to your students conveys the message that you are supporting their learning and that you care about them.

Respectful communications

Positive relationships encourage students' motivation and engagement in learning. Students need to feel that their teachers respect their views, opinions and interests. Give students space in your class to express themselves.

Positive environment

A positive environment will help your students to link the concepts and skills they are learning to their own experiences. Build fun and innovation into the things you do in your classroom. In other words, plan activities that create a sense of community so that your students have an opportunity to see the connections between what they already know and the new things they are learning, as well as have the time to enjoy being with you and the other students.

For example, in Vicky Duckworth's literacy class she drew on the literacies students used in their life outside the classroom to motivate learning. Indeed, it is generally thought that recognizing the literacies which students bring into the classroom is an effective strategy to facilitate teaching and learning because purposeful and meaningful learning builds and expands on students' prior knowledge and experience in order to shape and construct new knowledge, rather than seeing the learner as an empty vessel ready to be filled by the tutor. Learning is seen as a social activity embedded in particular cultures and contexts where assessment is based on students demonstrating their competence in achieving the specific learning outcomes. Demonstration of the achievement of these learning outcomes is situated in the students' real life and everyday practices. The teaching and learning resources can be developed by the learner to capture and give meaning to their experience, motivation and aspirations, or co-produced with the teacher (see McNamara 2007; Duckworth 2008, 2009), rather than arising from a pre-set curriculum.

Listening closely is also a key factor in establishing effective relationships with students. Below is a case study which offers an insight into the views of two adult students who were involved in an international participatory action research project. The purpose was for the educators to gain in-depth knowledge from two students who beat the odds by being highly successful in their academic pursuits as non-traditional adult students. This information can assist adult educators in transitioning marginalized adult students from basic skills courses into post-secondary education.

Activity 3.7

Consider what a good teacher–student relationship looks like and why you think these relationships matter.

Case study: Marie and Cynthia

Several years ago, two women embarked on a similar course. Marie, a single mother of three children, living in the United Kingdom, had ended her formal education at the age of 15. Cynthia, a married mother of two children, living in the United States, had dropped out of high school at the age of 16. Both struggled with basic academic skills. In spite of these barriers, both women enrolled in educational programmes to enhance their skills. This led to a transformation of both of their lives.

What advice do Marie and Cynthia have for educators who work with students with previous educational experiences similar to their own?

66 'If it had been a teacher I was used to as a child I would
have walked out. He never made me feel fake. He was
always happy to repeat things without rolling his eyes or

giving the look,' says Marie speaking about Bill, the first teacher she had when she entered the literacy program. Marie's words are powerful. As an **adult learner**, she feared the classroom. Her childhood memories caused a great deal of anxiety for her and Bill's patience and support kept her coming back. Marie lacked a social network that supported her in her education. As a single mother of three, she rarely had someone encouraging and cheering her on . . . One of the things that Cynthia appreciated about her educational experience was realizing she was capable of learning more than she expected.

(Johnson et al. 2010) **99**

Importantly, practitioners who nurture positive relationships with their students create classroom environments more favourable to learning and meet students' developmental, emotional and academic needs. Part of establishing supportive and productive links with learners is recognizing the way students can be categorized in terms of medical labels and the impact of this.

The medical model versus the social model of disability

Medical model

In a nutshell, the medicalization of disability locates the problems of disability within the individual rather than in society. People are disabled due to their individual impairments and therefore require medical interventions to provide them with the skills to adapt to society.

Social model

The social model of disability is a progressive **political concept** that opposes the medical model commonly used in the health professions. The social model is a concept which recognizes that some individuals have physical or psychological differences that can affect their ability to function in society. The social model suggests it is society, rather than the medical condition, that disables the individual with these physical or psychological differences. In other words, individuals with impairments are not disabled by their impairments but by the barriers that exist in society, which do not take their needs into account.

Attention Deficit Hyperactivity Disorder

Attention Deficit Hyperactivity Disorder, or ADHD as it is now commonly known, is a modern phenomenon. It can be very challenging to practitioners who often struggle to find strategies to engage and motivate these students with ADHD.

Students with ADHD may display the following behaviour:

- have difficulty remaining seated;
- fidget with hands and feet;
- may be easily distracted by visual or auditory stimuli in and outside the classroom;
- find it difficult to wait for turns in classroom discussions and other situations, such as practical tasks;
- have difficulty following directions and instructions;
- have difficulty in sustaining attention on class work or lecture;
- chatter continually to fellow classmates;
- have difficulty in doing class work quietly;
- interrupt or intrude when others are speaking;
- struggle to stay focused on a single task and shift from one task to another;
- do not seem to be listening when being spoken to;
- lose things like homework assignments or completed homework;
- may be disorganized and lack focused concentration to get a task completed.

However, the above behaviour could also be true of a high number of children and young people who, for example, are bored, immature, or lack the motivation to engage in the lesson and learn. Researchers who surveyed teachers found that factors such as class size influence the perceived incidence of ADHD (Glass and Wegar 2000). Worryingly, they also found that a high percentage of teachers support the use of medication, even when they do not believe ADHD to be a biological condition. This led Glass and Wegar (2000: 418) to conclude that 'the problem may lie in the educational system, not within the child'. We would suggest that understanding challenging behaviour in children and young people requires reference to a range of social and individual factors. We recognize that the labelling of children and young people with ADHD does not take place in a vacuum, but is instead a complex process of policy interests, funding pressures and professional discourses. There is an argument against medicating growing numbers of children and young people so that they can remain seated and robotic in class. Instead, perhaps the answer lies in making changes to the teaching and learning strategies we use in compulsory and post-compulsory education. As practitioners we need to stand outside our comfort zone and, rather than expecting children and young people to be disciplined and autonomous, we need to seek out innovative and meaningful support and guide students by modelling these behaviours in our own pedagogical practices. We need to take responsibility for teaching and recognize that some students will need more open guidelines than others, some will need repetition of instruction, some will need more extensive differentiation, and some will require concrete demonstration of concepts, which may mean drawing on students' interests, motivations and everyday practices, such as incorporating text messaging into the lesson, lyrics from songs, hobbies, and so on.

Because students with ADHD often have difficulty remaining motivated and focused, they need practitioners who are enthusiastic and who actively engage students in the learning process. They also need practitioners who are flexible and willing to try new ways to teach and assess. Along with flexibility, these students need practitioners with high expectations who believe that all students are capable of learning and reaching their potential.

Case study: Louise Losztyn

PGCE student teaching BTEC Subsidiary Diploma and National Diploma in Performance.

Units: Principles of Acting and Developing Voice for the Actor.

Establishing ground rules

For my first individual teach I decided to work coherently with my students in order to establish ground rules, as I knew from my observational and team teaching experiences that they could be a very rowdy bunch. A couple of the students have been identified with learning disabilities, which initially I found extremely challenging. They found it hard to focus on the lesson and caused the other learners to also lose focus and become distracted. In order to avoid the students feeling like I was disciplining them, I made the activity much more industry-centred, rather than discipline-centred. This surprisingly worked exceptionally well, as all of the students contributed positively and everyone agreed on the rules set. There were a few inappropriate comments primarily, such as 'alcohol at all times', but I made an immediate yet subtle point to shut these remarks down and a positive result was achieved.

During this activity I made a conscious effort to acknowledge the students' clear need for engaging in incessant communication with the outside world. Therefore, we agreed collaboratively that if the students kept their phones away on silent and did their work as expected, then I would allocate 2–3 minutes throughout the lesson where they could check their phones for any messages and texts. The students appeared to really respect me for granting them accessibility to their phones at given times, and I feel that this was a great way of incorporating and managing the use of phones in a positive way, rather than preventing the behaviour from occurring, often resulting in the students rebelling.

I also asked the students what they expected from me as I felt it was important to bestow them with the responsibility to acknowledge the necessities for success; the rule of 'Louise to know what she is doing' was established. I signed the rules alongside the rest of the students and assured them that if they kept their end of the bargain, then I would keep mine. For the first time since I have been on placement not one phone was visible throughout my whole three-hour lesson and all of the students were on time after their break.

I would definitely recommend establishing ground rules with new students for other trainee teachers and/or professionals, as it not only conferred classroom manageability on me, but it also generated a sense of trust, as it was confirmed to the students that I was 'on their side' and understood their needs, *if* they and *I* mutually conformed to the rules.

Conclusion

A practitioner's main drive should be the motivation of students. It goes without saying that, if students are not motivated during class, it not only affects their learning but their classroom discipline issues. However, teachers who have a real interest in their students plan and implement innovative lessons using a wide variety of teaching and learning strategies. The underlying factors in an individual's behaviour that challenges others may have a range of aetiologies and may be complex. Barriers to learning can also be located within the broader social and economic context. These barriers manifest themselves in different ways and may only become obvious when the learning cycle breaks down or/and when students exit the programme before completion. The key to preventing barriers from occurring is the effective monitoring and meeting of the different needs among your students. Great teachers inspire rather than coerce. Great teachers identify the reason that a lesson is being taught and then share it with their students. These teachers inspire their students through curiosity, challenge and relevancy.

Recommended reading

hooks, b. (1994) *Teaching to Transgress: Education as the Practice of Freedom.* New York: Routledge.

McLaren, P. and Leonard, P. (eds) (1993) *Paulo Freire: A Critical Encounter.* London: Routledge.

Reay, D., David, M.E. and Ball, S. (2005) *Degrees of Choice: Social Class, Race and Gender in Higher Education.* Stoke-on-Trent: Trentham Books.

Tedder, M. and Biesta, G.J.J. (2009) Biography, transition and learning in the lifecourse: the role of narrative, in J. Field, J. Gallacher and R. Ingram (eds) *Researching Transitions in Lifelong Learning.* London: Routledge.

References

Ball, S.J. (1981) *Beachside Comprehensive: A Case Study of Secondary Schooling.* Cambridge: Cambridge University Press.

Barnes, R. (1999) *Positive Teaching, Positive Learning.* London: Routledge.

Bowlby, J. (1969) *Attachment and Loss. Volume 1: Attachment.* New York: Basic Books.

Duckworth, V. (2008) *Getting Better Student Worksheets* (Adult Literacy Resources). Warrington: Gatehouse Books.

Duckworth, V. (2009) *On The Job: Car Mechanic Tutor Resources*, On The Job 14–19 Series. Warrington: Gatehouse Books.

Duckworth, V. and Cochrane, M. (2012) Spoilt for Choice, Spoilt by choice: Long-term consequences of Limitations Imposed by Social Background, *Journal of Education and Training*, 54(7) (forthcoming).

Freire, P. (1993) *Pedagogy of the Oppressed*. New York: Continuum.

Gardner, R., Cairns, J. and Lawton, D. (2000) *Education for Values: Morals, Ethics and Citizenship in Contemporary Teaching*. London: Kogan Page.

Glass, C. S. and Wegar, K. (2000) Teacher perceptions of the incidence and management of attention deficit hyperactivity disorder, *Education*, 121(2): 412–20.

Goffman, E. (1959) *The Presentation of Self in Everyday Life*. New York: Doubleday and Anchor Books.

Goffman, E. (1963) *Stigma: Notes on Management of Spoiled Identity*. London: Cox and Wyman.

Goodman, A. and Gregg, P. (eds) (2010) *The Importance of Attitudes and Behaviour for Poorer Children's Educational Attainment*. York: Joseph Rowntree Trust. Available at: http://www.jrf.org.uk/sites/files/jrf/poorer-children-education-summary.pdf.

Heider, F. (1958) *The Psychology of Interpersonal Relations*. New York: Wiley.

Johnson, C., Duckworth, V., McNamara, M. and Apelbaum, C. (2010) A tale of two adult students: from adult basic education to degree completion, *National Association for Developmental Education Digest*, 5(1): 57–67.

Kolb, D.A. (1984) *Experiential Learning: Experience as the Source of Learning and Development*. Englewood Cliffs, NJ: Prentice Hall.

Luttrell, W. (1997) *School-smart and Mother-wise: Working-class Women's Identity and Schooling*. New York: Routledge.

Maslow, M. (1954) *Motivation and Personality*. New York: Harper.

McNamara, M. (2007) *Getting Better*. Warrington: Gatehouse Books.

Reay, D. (2005) Beyond consciousness? The psychic landscape of class?, *Sociology*, 395: 911–28.

Reynolds, W.M. and Miller, G.E. (eds) (2003) *Handbook of Psychology: Educational Psychology* (7). Hoboken, NJ: John Wiley and Sons.

Rolfe, G., Freshwater, D. and Jasper, M. (2001) *Critical Reflection in Nursing and the Helping Professions: A User's Guide*. Basingstoke: Palgrave Macmillan.

Rosenthal, R. and Jacobson, L. (1992) *Pygmalion in the Classroom: Teacher Expectation and Pupils' Intellectual Development*, expanded edn. New York: Irvington.

Rosenthal, R., Rosnow, R.L. and Rubin, D.B. (2000) *Contrasts and Effect Sizes in Behavioral Research: A Correlational Approach.* Cambridge: Cambridge University Press.

Steedman, C. (1988) 'The mother made conscious': the historical development of primary school pedagogy, in M. Woodhead and A. McGrath (eds) *Family, School and Society.* London: The Open University.

Thomas, L., Bland, D. and Duckworth, V. (2012) Teachers as advocates for Widening Participation, Journal of Widening Participation and Lifelong Learning (forthcoming).

Weiner, B. (1986) *An Attributional Theory of Motivation and Emotion.* New York: Springer-Verlag.

Wlodkowski, R. J. (2008) *Enhancing Adult Motivation to Learn: A Comprehensive Guide for Teaching All Adults.* San Francisco: Jossey-Bass.

CHAPTER

4

The adolescent learner

By the end of the chapter you will be able to:

- understand why the 14–19 age range is a distinct learning phase;
- reflect on your own practice with 14- to 19-year-old students;
- identify strategies that will enable effective engagement and learning in the 14–19 classroom.

Introduction

Adolescence is an important transition point and a distinct developmental stage in its own right, being a time of major emotional, physical and neurological change. To meet the changing needs of students in the classroom, teachers need to be aware of the development of the young people they are working with. The transition of young students from primary to secondary school has rightly become an important focus for Key Stage 2 and 3 staff. Pupils are introduced to their new role as secondary school students gradually and staff from both settings work together to ensure a smooth transition during what can be a challenging time for children. The transition of students later in their school career from Key Stages 3 to 4 and post-16 study is not always as carefully managed and yet this is a significant period of change for those students. This period of transition could be seen as an opportunity for schools to rethink the curriculum, the classroom and the teaching pedagogy that underpins learning. Not only are Year 10 students experiencing significant physical developmental changes but the whole focus of their learning becomes outcome-driven. Target grades for each subject are often identified at the start of Year 10 (and Year 9 in an increasing number of schools where the Key Stage 4 learning has been extended) and the importance of learning for many students comes into sharp focus as they become increasingly aware of their abilities and limitations.

14- to 19-year-old students often express a growing demand for respect from their peers and the teachers they work with as they try to establish their own identity. Many students feel that teachers do not understand this desire (Blatchford 1996) and while the students increasingly see themselves as adults, their teachers may not always have the same perception of them, seeing adolescence as a time when students are more impulsive and likely to take greater risks without recognizing the long-term consequences of their behaviour. When discussing what it means to be an adult, students will often refer to the need to be heard and have some control over their lives and this may be difficult to manage in a classroom setting. The generation gap between teachers and students can add to the communication problem between the two (Bentley 1998) and, with students increasingly wanting to exert control over their own lives while staff feel the need to increase control over adolescent students, conflict is not unexpected. Lumby and Foskett sum up the dilemma by asking 'How can young people be offered the independence and choice they increasingly demand, and yet be protected from the ill effects of such independence which they themselves fear as well as desire?' (Lumby and Foskett 2007: 7).

All teaching needs to be creative and innovative and this is especially important when planning teaching and learning for the 14–19 age range. The model of good teaching made implicit by Ofsted relies on clear learning objectives which are explained and discussed at the start of the lesson, followed by activities that are appropriate for all students, engaging and well-paced, and a plenary at the end of the lesson designed to assess the quality of learning that has taken place. This same structure applies to the teaching of 14- to 19-year-olds. However, it is important to see the students not simply as children but as young adults and, as such, planning for learning needs to draw on both pedagogical and andragogical strategies to engage and support young adults in the classroom.

Pedagogy is based on the assumption that children need guidance and control in the classroom with their learning being dependent on the input of the teacher. Andragogy, on the other hand, identifies students as adults, who bring with them a wealth of experiences and self-motivation. In fact, both teaching and learning styles are relevant at all ages and this is most definitely the case with the 14–19 age range when students desperately want to be treated as adults but also need the guidance and structure provided by the teaching staff they are working with. This 'interface' between childhood and adulthood needs to be managed carefully to avoid the classroom becoming a 'battlefield' (Lumby and Foskett 2007).

Lesson planning for Key Stage 4 and 5 students needs to recognize the diversity of students that may be in any one classroom. As any Year 10 teacher will tell you, the range of physical developmental stages in one class can be huge, with some students, particularly those who have birthdays in the autumn term, on the verge of adulthood. Students may be increasingly self-motivated and feel confident drawing on their own life experiences. If learning does not give them the opportunity to make decisions, solve problems and draw on their own experience, some students may become increasingly frustrated with the uniform, teacher-dependent and outcome-focused delivery they may have experienced throughout their school life so far. Making learning relevant to the students' lives and allowing them the opportunity to identify with the learning taking place are key to avoid the often heard questions 'Why are we doing this?' and 'What has this got to do with the real world?' The transition from Key Stage 4 to 5 can be significant and most teachers would agree that students are often unprepared for the demands of post-16 learning and assessment.

While students are in this transitional, adolescent phase there is a need to scaffold learning closely until the students have developed the skills to move their own learning forward. Breaking down activities and assignments into manageable 'chunks' will allow students to manage their learning, targeting smaller goals which will then come together, in much the same way as you might complete a jigsaw. Beginning with corners, the underpinning essential knowledge and understanding should be added, much like completing the outside of the jigsaw, matching up the straight edges. At this point, students may then be ready to begin work on the complete picture, using the support and expertise of their teacher to enable them to identify where each piece fits. Given the variety of students and abilities in most 14–19 classrooms, the level of scaffolding needed to support students will vary and much depends on the skill of teachers to build effective relationships with their students, knowing when and how to support them and planning for individual needs and abilities in their classroom.

To ensure all 14–19 students have the opportunity to achieve to their full potential, schools need to prepare their students for the challenge of Key Stage 4 and 5 teaching and learning. Trainee teacher programmes would do well to consider the development of their teachers in training and prepare them for the very different classroom that they are likely to face when working with young adults.

Adolescent development

Imagine your new computer has just been delivered; you start to unpack the components and are soon surrounded by boxes, wires, cables and leads. The adolescent brain is a complex mix of components that have not yet been expertly put together to work effectively. In fact, scientists have discovered that there is a growth in synapses during the teenage years but they are not necessarily plugged in to the right portals or drives. The synapses are the leads and cables which make up your computer system but they take time to find their right role, just as you may find yourself plugging a lead in to a number of outputs until you find the right one. This growth in synapses along with the protective coating that surrounds them (myelin) enables the different sections of the brain to communicate with each other and myelination improves the communication speed between neurons. The important part of the brain which governs understanding and judgement and controls responses such as impulses and emotions is at the front of the brain, the prefrontal cortex. As adolescence progresses, the brain takes the mass of wiring and starts to remove or prune the synapses not needed and secure the connections required for the next 80 years. This process starts at the back of the brain and so, gradually, the different parts of the adolescent brain begin to work together. One of the last parts of the brain to be hooked up effectively, given that this rewiring process begins at the back, is the prefrontal cortex.

What this means for the young adult is that the part of the brain which controls impulses, helps to make reasoned choices and decisions and governs behaviour, the prefrontal cortex, is the last to be hooked up. This can make decision-making slow, clumsy and fraught with errors and confusion. Research in 2004 at the University of Pittsburgh concluded that processing speed reached maturity at age 15, inhibitory control at age 14, and working memory did not reach mature performance until the age of 19 (see Jarrett 2011). Adolescents will eventually get there, but in the meantime, teachers of the 14–19 age range have to manage young people with behaviour that is not always predictable, even to the teenagers themselves.

A further part of the brain that is well developed in adolescents is the component that is focused on pleasure and reward. The response to reward can be much bigger than expected and imaging has shown that small rewards do not trigger as much of a response as medium or larger rewards (Blakemore and Frith 2004). Again, this is likely to impact on how teenagers' behaviour is managed effectively in the classroom and no doubt explains why a simple 'well done' sticker no longer produces the delight that it does among younger students. Most schools will have in place a rewards and sanction policy designed to manage the behaviour of its students in a positive way. Given the changing outlook and attitudes of 14–19 students, it makes sense to consider how rewards may be incorporated for older students that are likely to motivate and be attractive. Rather than offering a certificate of merit, some schools now operate a 'bingo'-style system where students collect points and are able to trade in points for prizes. The range of prizes on offer can be quite imaginative: in one school, the class could bid for an end-of-term treat using their joint points total, with one Year 10 group opting for a takeaway pizza order for the whole class to enjoy one lunch time.

Another school displayed their rewards according to the number of points needed to claim them, in much the same way as a seaside bingo hall. The top prize was a bicycle which was proudly displayed in the reception area of the school in the same way that a prize car may be displayed in a shopping centre.

Identity and the struggle for independence

Erik Erikson (1968) famously coined the phrase 'identity crisis' to describe any change in direction or turning point in a person's life. However, for some adolescents the turning point may well turn into a crisis if they are not supported during this period of physical growth and cognitive change. The formation of identity was seen by Erikson as an important part of adolescence and this is the time when young people often begin to question who they are and what their role in life is or will be. This struggle for identity is often exhibited in a student's appearance, friendship groups, musical tastes, hobbies and interests. An outgoing student who enjoys socializing with friends at school and contributing to classroom discussion will often behave very differently at home. Many parents are often quite surprised to hear at parents' evenings about their quiet and sullen child at home who is chatty, friendly and outgoing at school, saying 'He tells us nothing about school.' Wanting to keep their emerging identity at school and among their peers to themselves is part of the struggle for independence. Trying out their identity away from the control of parents is an important developmental process for young adults and allows them to really achieve an identity that they are comfortable with and not one forced on them by the expectations of the adults around them. Expectations about appropriate forms of identity may add to the confusion some adolescents feel at this time; these expectations may be cultural, gender-related or sexual.

Whatever the identity struggles a student may face, the teacher's role should be one of support and understanding. School should be a place where identity and independence can be reflected on and Personal, Social and Health Education can provide the environment where students are able to develop and strengthen their identity and learn the skills needed to become independent successfully.

Common emotional health issues and the impact on learning

2011 has seen mental health rightly gain a degree of publicity and it is estimated that one in four of us will encounter a mental health problem of some kind during our lives and one in six do so at any one time. Forty-five per cent of GPs say stress and mental health issues will be the biggest health issue they will treat this year; nearly a quarter of disability in the UK is caused through mental ill health and treatment is the single most expensive cost to the NHS (Aviva 2012). The publication of the White Paper *No Health without Mental Health* (DH 2011) sets out the cross-government strategy that aims to mainstream mental health in England and improve standards of care, support and treatment. According to the White Paper, schools report significant benefits from the Targeted Mental Health in Schools programme. Adolescence is identified in the report as a distinct developmental stage in its own right and a period of increased risk taking which may increase the possibility of mental health problems developing.

Adolescence for some students may be characterized by a roller coaster of emotional, physical and psychological highs and lows. Promoting positive mental health among 14- to 19-year-olds is essential to protect them while at school or college and in the future as mental health issues which become apparent in adulthood invariably start in adolescence. The difficulty facing professionals working with young people is identifying what is a serious mental health concern in adolescence and what is a normal fluctuation in mood and behaviour, expected during this time of change. Defining a mental health problem often involves careful monitoring and recording of changes, whatever they may be. For some students, symptoms may be minor – a change in engagement and a withdrawal in the classroom. For other students, anxiety disorders may produce very animated and challenging behaviour. Physical symptoms may present quite obviously with a student who is not thriving and may be restricting food intake but, when mood is affected, a quiet student may simply 'disappear' in the classroom, taking little part in learning, a behaviour that may not at first raise any concerns among staff. What is important is that any behaviour that is starting to have a negative impact on a student's ability to function effectively in school or college for whatever reason is investigated quickly and carefully as early intervention is crucial to helping restore well-being in any individual experiencing mental health problems.

Common mental health disorders affecting adolescents are anxiety disorders and depression disorders. Anxiety disorders can manifest themselves in a variety of ways including phobias, nervous conditions and excessive worrying. Students may introduce rituals into their day to address the anxiety and for some it can be the start of a battle with obsessive compulsive disorder. Depression disorders are characterized by feelings of hopelessness and helplessness and, while we can all feel like this at one time or another, these feelings become intense and cause extreme disruption to normal life for depression sufferers.

Identifying students who are at risk of developing a serious mental health problem is never going to be easy, particularly when the time spent with one member of staff may be as short as one hour per week. The first indication of a problem emerging will probably be found in assessment records or in the classroom itself. If there is an unexpected dip in grades compared to previous performance and target data, it may well be wise to start observing the student in the classroom and noting any behavioural changes. Disruptive behaviour may well indicate an underlying problem, particularly if it is out of character. However, withdrawing from the lesson would similarly be a cause for concern if the student has previously engaged well with the teaching and learning taking place. Absenteeism is another indicator that the student is not engaging with his or her learning and this may of course be for a variety of reasons. If a pattern of absenteeism or persistent absenteeism emerges, then a one-to-one tutorial is most certainly called for to discuss issues and difficulties students may be having with their studies or any more serious problems they may be encountering.

Issues for teaching and learning

Given the challenges that students and teachers face in the 14–19 classroom, it makes sense to consider how to manage this transitional phase effectively and support students to enable them to engage and achieve.

When asked what makes a good teacher, 14–19 students often identify similar characteristics, including the following:

- they treat us with respect and courtesy;
- they trust us;
- they are friendly and interested in us;
- they have a sense of humour and can share a joke;
- they are firm and in control of the classroom;
- they make lessons fun and interesting;
- they treat everyone the same and do not have favourites.

Clearly there are different challenges for each teacher in different educational settings but the characteristics listed above have been identified by students in a range of schools and, given the consensus, it may well be worthwhile considering your own approach to teaching and learning and reflect on how well you meet some of the ideals the students agree on. The following case studies illustrate how some of the issues found in the classroom have successfully been approached and are based on real experience.

Creating an accessible, adult-like learning environment

Case study

A group of Year 10 GCSE students is dominated by boys who are showing little interest in the subject being taught. They are often complaining that they are being 'treated like kids', the subject is not relevant to them and they do not see why they are learning what they are being taught. When 14- to 19-year-olds say that they would like to be treated with respect, courtesy and be trusted, what they are asking for is to be treated like adults. This desire to be seen as adults while still needing to be protected and guided in their learning is common but not always easy to manage in the 14–19 classroom. The class in question were taught on a Wednesday afternoon for a double period of two hours. The subject was a vocational

BTEC and the room did have access to PCs. The students had one other lesson each week, on a Friday, in the morning, which was a single lesson.

It was important to consider how to make the learning seem more adult, with the responsibility for the lesson being put onto the students, giving them some say in the lesson structure and delivery style. This might not be as difficult to manage as it first seems. Using the school email system, the group received an email on Monday with an 'agenda' for the double lesson later in the week and the follow-on lesson on Friday attached. The agenda was effectively the learning objectives and outcomes for the two teaching slots, reworded to make them look businesslike and professional. Equipment required for the lesson was listed and any homework that was due in was identified. The homework reminder acted as a 'nudge' to the group and two web links that might help with the homework were also included.

Two or three students who were performing well and making good progress were invited to start the double lesson each week with a small activity suitable as a starter for the group and providing an introduction to the day's learning. This provided opportunities for the most able students to be stretched and challenged (having to teach their classmates really stretched their own understanding) and, again, the students were able to feel they had some control over the learning they were engaging with.

Activity 4.1

- Consider how you can create a more adult-like learning environment for your students. Make use of the data available to identify the most able students and provide appropriate stretch and challenge activities that do not simply ask students to answer more of the same type of questions.
- Ask students for their school email account addresses and set up a group email for the class. This can be used for agendas, reminders about homework, feedback on homework, support materials and recommended reading and email sites.

AGENDA

In Wednesday's lesson (date) we will be:

1. Looking at the stages in the recruitment and selection process
2. Comparing different job specifications to identify key characteristics
3. Comparing person specifications to identify key characteristics
4. Looking at the difference between a job specification and a person specification

You will need to bring:

1. Your class work file
2. An example of a job advert

In Friday's lesson (date) we will be:

1. Looking at different job adverts and identifying key characteristics
2. Drawing up an example job advert
3. Putting together the job specification and person specification for the job

You will need to bring:

1. Your class work file

Take a look at the BIZED website for more information about the recruitment and selection process

http://www.bized.co.uk/learn/business/hrm/employ/recruit/student.htm

Planning for active learning

Estimates suggest that up to one third of young people are not actively engaged in the classroom (Ross 2009) and this will inevitably impact on levels of achievement and success beyond the classroom. Teachers need to focus on creating an effective learning environment rather than a teaching environment. What this means in practice is identifying strategies in the classroom that will allow students to learn actively and engage fully with their learning. An active scheme of work will identify teaching objectives for the lesson with appropriate outcomes (evidence of learning) from which the quality of learning can be assessed but, importantly, the scheme should also identify a range of activities that will allow students to engage and produce outcomes in a creative and enjoyable way.

Case study

A group of A-level students were struggling to understand how the nature of research would impact on the research methods chosen by the person conducting the research. Half of the students in the group of 16 were asked to pick a research method to look at in more detail (they picked their research method out of a hat). Guidance was given which included appropriate references and web sites to visit for further information. The second half of the class were given a research proposal and asked to read through the research idea and consider how they might go about collecting data.

A double lesson was set aside for the 'speed dating' activity, during which time the students sat facing each other for three minutes while the method of data collection that had been researched by their classmate was explained and questions could be asked about the method. The student looking for a suitable research method for his or her proposal would move from one 'date' to the next; at the end of the allocated time, the student who had been listening to the descriptions of each method of data collection had to decide on a suitable method for the proposal.

The timing of this activity was important to maintain pace and engagement and experience has shown that three minutes works well for each date. While students were discussing each research method, background music was played to provide a 'cover' for discussions. Using music in this way encourages students to talk to each other without the embarrassment of being overheard by others in the room. At the end of the speed dating, the results were shared with the group and those who had listened to the description and explanation of each research method were asked to vote on which mini-presentation they felt worked best and had enabled them to develop their knowledge and understanding of the research method. The winning date received a simple certificate, congratulating them on their mini-presentation and research skills, along with a small prize.

Activity 4.2

Consider the syllabus you are teaching and timetable slots where it might be possible to develop active learning opportunities for your class. This type of lesson will need some careful planning but once the format has been delivered, you may be surprised how easy it is to provide similar active learning lessons every two to three weeks.

Creating reflective students

Too often students receive their assessed work and do not engage with the feedback at all, looking for the grade or mark received at the end of their work and completely ignoring the comments and feedback provided throughout their work and the suggestions for improvement at the end. To encourage students to engage with the assessment process and make assessment for learning really work for you and your students, consider leaving the final grade or mark for the piece of work off your feedback and ask the students to read the comments you have made and gauge from your comments what grade the work received.

Another way to encourage students to reflect on their own learning is to get students to grade their work themselves when they submit it. They can then compare your comments and grade with how they felt they had worked. Encourage students to measure their performance against their target grade for the subject: are they underperforming? If so, what are they going to do to improve their performance and hit their target?

Example of an active scheme of work

Week	Aim	Objectives	Outcomes	Assessment	Resources
Unit introduction	Students will understand the unit content and its assessment including Cognitive and Developmental Psychology and Research Methods.	To establish the structure of the topic and its assessment criteria.	Students will receive a topic booklet outlining the objectives of each lesson throughout the course of the topic including details of assessment.	Students will demonstrate an understanding of how the topic will be delivered to them and how they will be assessed.	Video of Clive Wearing-http://www.youtube.com/watch?v=Vwigmktix2Y PowerPoint Presentations Worksheets AQA A Specification Up-to-date newspaper reports
1 5 × 1 hour lessons	Students will develop knowledge and understanding of the multi-store model of memory (MSM). Students will know and understand the basic components of investigation design.	Students will be able to describe the MSM and explain the terms of encoding, capacity and duration. They will be able to identify the differences in encoding, capacity and duration between STM and LTM. (AO1) Students will be able to give definitions for independent and dependent variables and repeated and independent measures (AO1). They will also be able to create hypotheses, carry out simple research and generate and interpret data (AO3); applying it to the MSM (AO2).	Students will:- • draw a visual representation of the MSM (V) • participate in a class experiment (K) where they will highlight the variables and determine the experimental design • display data and apply results of various experiments to theories of memory • read and analyse accounts of research into encoding • evaluate research into the encoding, capacity and duration of memory • participate in class-competitive games to summarize lesson/topic (A) • in groups, analyse research into the capacity of STM and feed back to the group (A) • create a flow chart detailing the methodology of research into the duration of LTM (V) • complete written summaries of lesson content on supplied worksheets	Assessment of initial understanding of topics will occur using prompting questions prior to delivery or with interactive starter activities. Students will assess their own written classwork against correct examples displayed by the teacher; worksheets will also be collected in regularly and marked, recorded and handed back with feedback detailing strengths and methods of improvement. The achievement of lesson objectives will be also partly assessed using targeted summarizing and revisiting questions alongside class competitive games. Students' verbal contributions will be recorded and monitored and will aid the quality of feedback given when marking classwork or homework.	S&C extension work Newspaper reports will be handed to students and they will be instructed to suggest possible psychological links. Cross-curricular links • *Maths/Statistics:* Displaying and interpreting data • *Literacy:* Writing in continuous prose (QWC) • *Science:* Creating and testing hypotheses • *Social Studies:* Understanding how patients deal with memory problems
Differentiation	Scaffolding will be concentrated on weaker students during pair/group/individual work with the use of supplementary prompting questions and retrieval cues. A variety of learning styles relevant to the VAK inventory will be addressed throughout the week. Questions in Q&A sessions will be targeted relating to ability and worksheets with supplementary sub-questions will be handed to weaker students. Groups will be sorted into similar ability to allow higher ability groups to work on more difficult accounts of research.				
Homework	Students will compare their topic booklet with the specification from the AQA website and be ready to discuss what they have found in lesson.				

STM = short-term memory; LTM = long-term memory; V = visual; A = ; K = kinaesthetic.

Case study

One group of AS students were struggling to improve their writing and homework tasks were not completed in enough detail, or failed to address the assessment outcomes from the specifications, particularly the need to evaluate their writing and draw appropriate conclusions. A generic feedback sheet was put together to provide clear guidance on what was done well and where the students needed to improve. Recommended reading and support were included and students were expected to make a comment themselves on what they would now do to improve their writing. The feedback was emailed back to students, enabling them to easily follow suggested web links, and students were asked to complete their reflection and send the feedback to their teacher. This made the reflection process a formal part of assessment; both teacher and student identified targets for improvement with appropriate strategies to achieve the targets and, importantly, these targets had been shared.

Activity 4.3

Make time to review how students receive feedback on their work. Do you provide sufficient detail as to how the work may be improved? Devise a feedback sheet that has space for your comments and recommendations to improve but also has an area for student reflection, target setting and next steps strategies to improve.

Making learning relevant

Learner engagement can be improved by using strategies that place the learner at the centre of the teaching and learning process and clearly identify why the learning is taking place by referring to exam specifications and assessment criteria. Learning has to be meaningful for students to really immerse themselves in the process and lessons can engage students even further by making learning active and applied. Make learning accessible and meaningful by making use of local resources to illustrate and engage students. Active learning lessons will provide opportunities for students to research a concept or issue and develop their knowledge and understanding either independently or as part of a small group. Students should then be encouraged to explain what they have discovered to their peers and their teacher. Students and staff should instantly see the difference in the classroom; a well-managed active lesson can often leave teachers wondering what *they* should be doing as students are busy with the tasks they have been set.

Case study

A class of mixed-ability Year 11 students were ready to look at the recruitment and selection process in business studies. The homework set the previous lesson was relatively simple – each student was given a key term to research at home and produce a simple definition suitable for the whole class to use in their unit dictionary. A carousel activity had been planned for the lesson and students had been arranged into mixed-ability groups of five students, based on their specific needs and talents. Students were asked to sit according to a seating plan at their 'home table' and the first activity they were expected to do in their group was explain to the rest of their group the key term they had researched.

Each member of the home group was given a number and a sticky label on which to put their first name and number. Around the room, five carousel activities had been set up which covered a range of learning objectives – the objective for each activity was clearly displayed on each table; for example, table one had the objective 'you will be able to describe each stage in the recruitment and selection process using a simple flow diagram'. On the table was provided text books and example recruitment policies from some of the larger, local businesses, along with sample flow diagrams illustrating the stages a Human Resources department in a business would go through to fill a vacancy. All the number ones from each group sat together and made notes on the stages in the recruitment and selection process. Each chunk of learning was carefully timed using a simple timer on the white board and background music was played to mask discussion and encourage all students to contribute without embarrassment.

After ten minutes, students had to return to their home group and then, in turn, teach their group what they had learned. Students knew that they would have to teach their group the new knowledge and/or skill they had learnt and this encouraged them to make sure they really understood clearly what they had to learn. The number ones began the mini-teach by providing an overview of each stage in the recruitment process, starting with the exit interview and finishing with the induction of new staff.

The teacher's role during each of the mini-teach sessions was to manage the timing of each session, which is crucial to the success of this type of activity or students may soon move off task, but also the teacher should carefully monitor the progress of each group and individual team members. After the mini-teach activities, each group was given one of the carousel activities on which to prepare a poster and present back to the whole class. A simple plenary returned to the key terms that students had been asked to research at home and had come across in the lesson. Students were asked to complete a quick written definitions quiz to check understanding.

Learning was made relevant by using the local newspaper as a resource for job advertisements. Learning objectives on each of the carousel stations were linked to assessment objectives from the specifications being followed, making it clear why the lesson content was being taught. Learning was also differentiated as students were assigned an activity according to their ability. For example, carousel activity one required knowledge and understanding only and was suitable for all abilities, hence the least able student in each group was assigned this task (group member one). Carousel activity five required students to consider a job advert, identify problems with the advert and suggest how the advert could be improved. This activity required students to demonstrate higher-level skills such as application and evaluation, making it suitable for the most able student in each group (group member five).

Activity 4.4

Local newspapers can be an invaluable source of material for your lessons. Writing is accessible and appropriate for the 14–19 learner and news articles refer to local issues, places, businesses and organizations which students can recognize and relate to. Consider how you might make learning relevant for your classes by using the local community and businesses as a source of material and exemplars in your teaching.

The return of the effort grade

Sports psychology has identified the importance of rewarding effort when attempting to motivate sports men and women. The same is true for the classroom and particularly 14–19 students. Given their need for praise and reward, students whose academic performance is not as it should be may become increasingly disengaged and demotivated with feedback that consistently highlights their underperformance. The increasingly common practice of using target grades to identify under-achievement does little to motivate students who have been receiving the same feedback month after month. What can be praised in all students, however, regardless of ability, is the level of effort a student has put into an activity or piece of work.

> **Case study**
>
> Ian was constantly underperforming compared to the target grade C he had been predicted to achieve in his GCSE. Despite the advice in his feedback on how his work could be improved, he became disengaged and resigned to failing the subject. After one particularly enjoyable group learning lesson, students were awarded grades based on their levels of participation and effort. Ian received a grade A and was delighted. A 'postcard of praise' was sent home to let his parent know about the excellent attitude to learning he had demonstrated in this particular lesson; no mention was made of his poor academic performance which had failed to reach the target grade predicted. The impact on Ian's attitude to learning was almost immediate and he was keen to put more effort into his learning and made use of the next steps web links that were provided to all students in the class when they received their next piece of work back.

Building effective relationships

Students often report that teachers who have positive relationships with the young people they teach are the same teachers who enjoy teaching and focus on creating a positive classroom environment (Russell et al. 2005). It would therefore seem that it is how students *perceive* their teachers that carries influence over whether they then engage with the teaching and learning taking place. Members of staff who appear to care for their students' welfare, are innovative and creative within the classroom, and focus on creating a learner-friendly environment for their students will be more likely to develop effective student engagement than teachers who do not display an interest, and do not focus on interesting pedagogy for their students. Learners in this age group will also engage better when they see themselves as part of a small community of students – for example, the A-level sociology group. Providing opportunities to develop the community both in and outside the classroom will strengthen that group identity and encourage engagement in the lesson and beyond. Consider creating an online community for your students to discuss their progress and difficulties. Use Twitter to provide valuable links to wider reading and discussion and useful reminders to students – for example, what homework is due when. Make use of Facebook to similarly engage students beyond the school/college gates. Groups can be set up using careful controls and open only to those to whom you grant access, thereby avoiding any online safety concerns you may have. Fostering small communities of students in this way can provide important opportunities for students to identify with their peers and develop attachment to the staff they are working with.

Building effective relationships with your students, whatever their age, is essential and teachers need to empathize with the challenges young people face in every aspect of their lives. Being a 'Peter Pan' in the classroom, identifying and acknowledging young people's culture, experiences and interests will reap rewards when building these important relationships. Many a female trainee teacher has spoken of the rewards they have experienced in the classroom when they have taken the time to research and follow the local football teams. This has been evident in a classroom with 14- to 19-year-old boys who have become increasingly disengaged from their studies.

Activity 4.5

Make use of a student profile sheet to gather information about each student's needs and abilities, hobbies and interests and their aspirations for life beyond the school gates. Not only can this make personalizing learning more effective but information about hobbies, for example, can be used to devise activities which draw on this information. Add to this profile any information held on file regarding special educational needs and add in numeracy and literacy levels if appropriate for the age range.

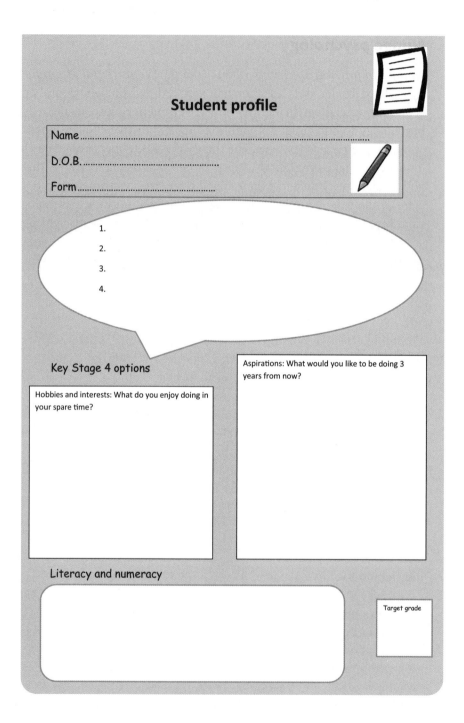

Student profile

Name..

D.O.B..

Form..

1.

2.

3.

4.

Key Stage 4 options

Hobbies and interests: What do you enjoy doing in your spare time?

Aspirations: What would you like to be doing 3 years from now?

Literacy and numeracy

Target grade

Nudge psychology

Nudge: Improving Decisions about Health, Wealth, and Happiness by Richard Thaler and Cass Sunstein (2008) draws on behavioural and economic psychology to identify how governments may consider using psychology to encourage the public to make positive choices when it comes to their everyday lives. The theory discusses how people may be 'nudged' to make the right decisions rather than trying to 'shove' them and Thaler and Sunstein's book has influenced governments on both sides of the Atlantic to consider how government may use psychology to induce the public to make choices that will benefit themselves personally and the economy as a whole. The Behavioural Insights Team or 'Nudge Unit' is now an established UK government department which aims to identify how the public can be nudged into making the right choices for the economy and their own health and well-being rather than being forced to do the right thing using negative consequences. Using behavioural theory is nothing new in the classroom. Operant conditioning is the theory which underpins positive behaviour management: students for some time have been rewarded for positive behaviour and school policies have in place a scale of sanctions intended to deter negative behaviour.

Nudge psychology may be adapted successfully for the classroom. Some may argue that it is effectively spoon feeding; however, when approached in a structured way, students should eventually develop the skills they need to feed themselves. In the classroom, teachers need to be nudging students to make the right choices rather than the wrong ones. In practice, this means that, rather than suggesting students read a particular piece of writing or follow up a reference in a journal, teachers provide extracts and possibly electronic links to the reading they would like their students to do.

Feedback needs to be carefully focused on the positives (two ticks) with one suggestion as to how work can be improved (the wish). The wish needs to identify clearly what students need to do to improve their work and provide a strategy for them to follow. This may include a link to a useful website where students can access further subject knowledge or a critique that would enhance their writing, available at the click of a mouse. Providing electronic feedback makes the 'nudge' even more effective as students can easily follow a hyperlink to the further reading they have been asked to do. Electronic feedback also provides the opportunity for the teacher to personalize feedback relatively easily and removes any stigma that may be attached to feedback in the classroom. Electronic feedback can tick another box for the 14–19 learner; making their learning more 'grown up'. Submitting and accessing work and feedback online is becoming the norm in the HE sector.

Teaching girls and boys

The differing success of girls and boys in different classroom environments has been the subject of much research of late. Opinion seems to support the teaching of girls in single-sex groups to develop their risk-taking skills and resilience. While such a structure may not be possible within the constraints of your school or college, it is possible to make use of this research in your own classroom by using group work and putting students into single-sex groups for an activity. Research has shown that if young people feel relaxed and positive, they are more likely to learn (Klem and Connell 2009).

Case study

A class of mixed-ability and mixed-sex Year 11 students was dominated by a small group of loud and boisterous male students. During a group carousel activity, the students were deliberately grouped in single-sex teams to complete the challenge. One group of girls contained three students who were consistently on the margins of the lesson, reluctant to contribute and acutely aware of their peers in the classroom whom they felt were judging every comment they made. Gemma, Vanessa and Rachel were placed in an all-female group for the lesson and while students were working on each activity, music was played to mask their conversations and encourage participation. Without doubt, the girls were more animated and interested in the activity and engagement was significantly improved. This same model was used for future group work and the girls' confidence soared over the term.

If you want your daughter to be a high-flying businesswoman or banker, send her to a single-sex school. This is the startling conclusion drawn from new research charting the complex relationship between gender and risk-taking.

Next month's edition of the Economic Journal *carries the results of an experiment by two economists at the University of Essex. Alison Booth and Patrick Nolen devised a series of questions for 260 male and female pupils that were designed to measure their appetite for risk. The pupils, from eight state single-sex and coeducational schools in Essex and Suffolk, were asked to choose between a real-stakes lottery and a sure bet. Option 1 guaranteed they won £5, while option 2 entered them in a lottery in which they would flip a coin and receive £11 if the coin came up heads or £2 tails.*

The economists found that, on average, girls were 16% less likely than boys to opt for the lottery. But significantly, they found that girls in coed schools were 36% less likely to select the lottery than their male peers. The findings appear to confirm the long-held view that males have a greater appetite for risk than females and go some way to indicating that this may be down to the environment in which a young person grows up. Girls at single-sex schools were also willing to invest more in a hypothetical risky investment than coed female and all-male pupils.

Activity 4.6

Observe and record the level of participation in your classroom and pay particular attention to differing levels of engagement among girls and boys. Consider devising group work which will allow students to work in single-sex groups and, again, observe levels of engagement. Make use of a simple lesson evaluation during your plenary to gauge the students' response to the changes you have made.

Recommended reading

Blakemore, S. and Frith, U. (2004) *The Learning Brain: Lessons for Education.* Oxford: Blackwell.

Coch, D., Fischer, K. W. and Dawson, G. (2010) *Human Behaviour, Learning, and the Developing Brain: Typical Development.* New York: Guilford Press.

Ginnis, P. (2002) *Teacher's Toolkit: Raise Classroom Achievement with Strategies for Every Learner.* Bancyfelin, Wales: Crown House Publishing.

Smith, J. and Gilbert, I (2010) *The Lazy Teacher's Handbook: How Your Students Learn More When You Teach Less.* Bancyfelin: Crown House Publishing.

Useful websites

http://www.english-teaching.co.uk/learninglearning.htm
Free resources from Paul Ginnis are available here to help you reflect on and improve your own practice.

http://www.geoffpetty.com
Geoff Petty provides a range of ideas and strategies to make learning active and enjoyable.

References

Aviva (2012) *The Aviva Health of the Nation Index.* Available at: http://www.aviva.co.uk/library/pdfs/health/hotn-spring-2012-gen4421.pdf.

Bentley, T. (1998) *Learning Beyond the Classroom: Education for a Changing World.* London: Routledge.

Blakemore, S. and Frith, U. (2004) *The Learning Brain: Lessons for Education.* Oxford: Blackwell.

Blatchford, P. (1996) Pupils' views on school work and school from 7–16 years, *Research Papers in Education,* 11(3): 263.

Coch, D., Fischer, K.W. and Dawson, G. (2010) *Human Behaviour, Learning, and the Developing Brain: Typical Development.* New York: Guilford Press.

DH (Department of Health) (2011) *No Health without Mental Health.* Available at: http://www.dh.gov.uk.

Erikson, E. (1968) *Identity: Youth and Crisis.* New York: Norton.

Jarrett, C. (2011) *The Rough Guide to Psychology.* London: Rough Guides Ltd.

Jarvis, M. (2005) *The Psychology of Effective Learning and Teaching.* Cheltenham: Nelson Thornes.

Klem, A.M. and Connell, J.P. (2009). Relationships matter: linking teacher support to student engagement and achievement, *Journal of School Health,* 74(7): 273.

Lumby, J. (2011). Enjoyment and learning: policy and secondary school students' experience in England, *British Educational Research Journal,* 37(2): 247–64.

Lumby, J. and Foskett, N. (2007) *14–19 Education: Policy, Leadership and Learning.* London: Sage Publications.

McCormick, C. B. and Pressley, M. (1997) *Educational Psychology: Learning, Instruction, Assessment.* Harlow: Longman.

Ross, A. (2009) Disengagement from education among 14–16 year olds. Available at: http://www.education.gov.uk/publications/standard/publicationDetail/Page1/DCSF-RR178 [Accessed 3 January 2012].

Russell, V.J., Ainley, M. and Frydenberg, E. (2005) Schooling issues digest: student motivation and engagement. Available at: http://www.dest.gov.au/sectors/school_education/publications_resources/schooling_issues_digest/schooling_issues_digest_motivation_engagement.htm# [Accessed 3 January 2012].

Thaler, R. and Sunstein, C. (2008). *Nudge: Improving Decisions about Health, Wealth, and Happiness.* New Haven, CT: Yale University Press.

Wolfe, P. and ASCD (2010) *Brain Matters: Translating Research into Classroom Practice,* 2nd edn. Alexandria, VA: Association for Supervision and Curriculum Development.

CHAPTER

5

Adult students

By the end of this chapter you will be able to:

- understand the development of adult education in England;
- consider teaching pedagogies specific to adult students;
- recognize a range of theories to support your understanding of adult behaviours;
- implement a range of strategies to manage, reduce or prevent unwanted adult behaviours.

Introduction

This chapter will allow the reader to explore a range of theories and strategies for teaching adults. Adults are among the most rewarding of students to teach; they are diverse, interesting, enquiring and hardworking. They can also be fearful, lack confidence and be disaffected. Not all adult students are in the classroom by choice; some are required to attend by their employers and many others are in the classroom through a lack of viable alternatives. Motivating, engaging and purposeful sessions are three of the key underpinning principles in the management of adult learning. Adult students are not easily defined, as is explored below, and differing definitions apply across age, phase and level of learning. For the purpose of this chapter, **adult learners** are defined as learners over the age of 21 or who have returned to education after a gap in their education chronology.

What is an adult learner?

The term adult learner is in itself problematic – what is an adult and when do we become an adult? There are a number of ways to define adulthood, such as chronological age or physiological milestones. Age-related milestones are complex and often determined by culture and attitude. The age of criminal responsibility in England, for example, is 10 years, yet in Norway it is 15 and 18 in Belgium. The age of majority in England, the legal term used to define the age at which you are classified as an adult and therefore, able to take decisions in your own right, free of parental or guardian interference, is 18.

Physiological changes, such as puberty, are fixed developmentally and not by a fixed age, although there are clearly norm continuums. It is useful to think of these types of changes as stages. The World Health Organization defines adolescents as those who are between the ages of 10 and 19, 'youths' between 15 and 24 and 'young people' between 10 and 24. Developmental theories apply to the ordered and significant changes that occur during an individual's lifetime, although Keenan's (2002) principle of multi-directionality maintains there is no single 'normal' path for development. Erik Erikson, a developmental psychologist and psychoanalyst, developed a psychosocial development based on eight stages of life from birth to death:

1 *Infancy*: birth to 18 months
2 *Early childhood*: 2–3 years
3 *Pre-school*: 3–5 years
4 *School age*: 6–11 years
5 *Adolescence*: 12–18 years
6 *Young adulthood*: 19–40 years
7 *Middle adulthood*: 40–65 years
8 *Maturity*: 65 to death

Each stage is influenced by important events and based on conflict. Young adulthood (19–40), for example, is rooted in the conflict between intimacy and isolation, and the need to form intimate relationships.

Success results in intimacy and failure in isolation (which can be long-lasting). In middle adulthood (41–65) the focus of the conflict is between 'generativity': concern and guidance for the next and future generations (and, in the wider sense, the ability to produce or originate something) and stagnation. Success at this stage is often characterized by high levels of productivity and satisfaction is attained through accomplishment or by useful contribution to the next generation. Failure often results in a withdrawal from, or shallow involvement with, the world. Maturity (65 to death) sees a conflict between ego integrity (fulfilment and self-acceptance) and despair. This stage can be characterized by wisdom, satisfaction and feelings of belonging and 'wholeness', or lead to despair, through realization of a personal lack of achievement and contribution. This sense of despair can deepen as the individual realizes there is insufficient time to rectify the situation.

It is the ego that acts as the driving force in human development and personality. Conflicts often result in identity crisis, a time when the individual lacks direction and may be confused or uncertain and unfulfilled. The existential question of 'Who am I?' is often a complicated aspect of adult students. In vocational programmes such as nursing or teaching this question of 'Who am I?' is often resolved during the development of a vocational or professional persona. Trainee teachers are asked to consider 'what type of teacher they would like to be' during the induction phase, often through reflecting on their own experiences of teachers – the good and bad. Although identity crisis can lead to negative outcomes, such as the isolation of young adulthood or the despair of maturity, it often leads to positive changes and thus resolution. While teachers are not, and should not, attempt to be psychologists, therapists or counsellors, awareness of the 'fragility' of some adult students is crucial. Supportive environments based on trust and encouragement are essential for maximizing successful outcomes for these students.

Thus, the complex range of milestones, whether developmental or chronological, illustrates the blurring of the boundaries between the teaching of children and adolescents, and adolescents and adults. The emergence of 14–19 as a distinct phase during the late 1990s and early 2000s spans both compulsory and post-compulsory education. The distinction between the two has been complicated following the gradual *de facto* elongation of education, enshrined in law following the

2008 Skills and Education Act, which increased the age of participation in education or training for young people from 16 to 17 in 2013 and 18 in 2015.

Expectations of participation in learning beyond the compulsory school age are not new. The Crowther Report *15–18*, written in 1959 for the Ministry of Education by Geoffrey Crowther (CACE 1959), recommended extending compulsory education from 15 to 16. This report also made reference to a recommendation of the 1944 Education Act 'that there should be compulsory part-time attendance at county colleges up to the age of 18 for all who have left school before then' (1959). Increased participation rates of all ages, including mature students within both further education (FE) and higher education (HE) increased dramatically from the 1970s onwards leading to what has been referred to as the **massification** of HE, where participation across all groups increased significantly.

Participation rates in higher education

For the purpose of HE statistical reporting, mature students are defined as those aged over 21. There is also widespread recognition of 'non-traditional mature students', defined as those being over the age of 25 and who have experienced a gap in their education chronology. The development of the Access movement during the 1970s and a widening participation agenda, targeting those from low participation communities and disadvantaged groups, led to a significant increase in mature students accessing HE. The numbers of mature students enrolling onto full-time undergraduate programmes doubled between the mid-1980s and the mid-1990s. Despite this, the percentage of students from non-traditional and disadvantaged groups continues to be significantly lower than those from higher socio-economic backgrounds, regardless of age. Young participants (entrants aged 18–19) to HE increased from 30 per cent in the mid-1990s to 36 per cent in 2010. Those applicants living in the most advantaged areas had a participation rate of 1 in 2, compared to less than 1 in 5 for young people living in the most disadvantaged areas (HEFCE 2010). The decline in overall application rates, particularly for those students aged 40 or over, is worrying – even more so when one considers these students may be the last generation to have left school without a mass expectation of higher education qualifications. A greater range of initiatives will be required to encourage more mature students into higher education at a time of spiralling costs for all education. Accelerated degrees – those delivered in two years instead of three, for example, have proved popular with mature students, with a participation rate of 66 per cent compared to younger entrants' participation at 36 per cent. Part-time degree courses remain popular for mature students:

> 66 HESA data for 2008–09 show that part-time students are much more likely to be mature; the mean age of part-time students studying for a first degree is 32.9 years (studying at an intensity of 50 per cent or more) or 34.7 years (studying at a lower intensity). This compares with a mean age of 20.4 years for full-time students studying for a first degree.
>
> *(HEFCE 2011)* 99

University application rates for all students aged over 21 dropped in 2011 with mature applications down by 5.7 per cent (UCAS 2011). However, following the introduction of higher university fees, the figures for 2012 indicate a decrease in applications across *all* age groups. The category with the largest decrease in applications is mature students, down a significant and worrying 25.2 per cent.

By age	2011	2012	Diff (+/−)	Diff (%)
17 and under	2940	2914	−26	−0.9
18	103201	93713	−9488	−9.2
19	36622	30068	−6554	−17.9
20	8921	7130	−1791	−20.1
21	4754	3936	−818	−17.2
22	3773	3429	−344	−9.1
23	3164	2585	−579	−18.3
24	2492	2056	−436	−17.5
25 to 29	6930	5499	−1431	−20.6
30 to 39	6131	4898	−1233	−20.1
40 and over	2886	2159	−727	−25.2
Total	**181814**	**158387**	**−23427**	**−12.9**

Source: UCAS (2012)

Widening participation to higher education for mature students was, until recently, a highly successful and highly visible feature of university education. The postwar discourse on education centred on improving equality of education opportunities. This was enshrined in government policy, such as the Robbins Report (1963). This report marked a defining point in university education and served as a pivotal force in the expansion of universities and acceptance of the 'Robbins principle' that admission to university should be based on the applicant's ability and attainment rather than social position.

History and purpose of adult education

There is a long and respected tradition of adult learning in the UK, evidencing a clear demand for education beyond the compulsory age and a demand for education beyond that prescribed by the state. The Society for Promoting Christian Knowledge, which encouraged adults to learn to read, was established in 1699 and Samuel Fox and William Singleton are widely reputed to have started the first 'adult school' in Nottingham in 1798. A gradual increase in schools from the 1850s was in some places coupled with an increase in the breadth of the curriculum. Joseph Sturge's Severn Street School included evening classes in 'arithmetic, geography and grammar' (Smith 2004). In addition, many charitable concerns organized lectures specifically targeting the working classes, such as those recorded by William Johnson Fox (1786–1864). Fox's (1846) book *Lectures: Addressed Chiefly to the Working Classes* comprised 20 lectures, with titles ranging from 'On moral power and money power', 'Mental freedom' and 'Mental slavery' to 'Robert Burns, the first poet of the poor'. The collection offers an insight into the social and moral drivers permeating Victorian society. These principles underpinned education for the working classes, be they adults or children, the overarching purpose of which was that of improving moral standards. One way in which this could be achieved was through developing the ability of the working classes to read and understand scripture.

Thus, many educators saw the role of education as a means of maintaining the status quo, a tool of the state apparatus rather than as a revolutionary machine or a means of overcoming preordained class determinism. The primary function of these early adult education classes differed, but many philanthropists such as Hannah More (1745–1833), who wrote a series of short narratives known collectively as the 'Cheap Repository Tracts', called for a conservative approach enforcing the existing social order, 'teaching them that joy in heaven was the recompense for deprivation on earth' (Smith 2002).

As with definitions of adult or mature students, the *purpose* of adult education is also unclear. The current uneasy compromise appears to be that of a combination of a relatively narrow range of opportunities for upskilling or reskilling, generally vocational in nature, offered predominantly through further education colleges and universities, and a wider range of courses including those for self-fulfilment and enjoyment offered through adult education classes.

Further education, in particular, has been seen as a second chance for students for whom compulsory schooling failed, or for those who were un-engaged. From the 1970s, Access courses for mature non-traditional students grew in response to the widening participation agenda. A highly successful initiative, the courses specifically target mature students, are nationally recognized and prepare the learner for study at HE. The principle of widening education, while still acknowledged, will be difficult to maintain, given the funding reduction of 25 per cent for the FE sector for 2011–15 (BIS 2010). Although mature students 'aged 24 or over studying qualifications at Level 3 or above [will have access to] income-contingent loans' (BIS 2010: 2), the focus of support remains on young students and those students without basic literacy and numeracy skills. The use of charitable organizations and philanthropy to promote social causes features strongly in the current government's agenda, with its emphasis on community, duty and responsibility and of the 'big society'. While philanthropy is in itself a laudable action, a more cynical view could suggest the focus on volunteers, community empowerment and social action is an attempt to mask the extent and severity of the spending cuts.

As the government gradually erodes the financial support available for adult students, beyond that of ensuring that adult workers are educated to basic minimum standards in information and communications technology (ICT), numeracy and literacy, adult education risks becoming an exclusive commodity, restricted to those with the means to fund themselves. As the current austerity measures are likely to remain for the foreseeable future, the personal value of lifelong learning will continue to be in conflict with the costs of providing and accessing such learning.

The introduction of tuition fees has had an impact on student enrolment behaviour although, over time, this may be seen as an exception rather than a downward trend. There may be other unintended consequences of tuition fees on student behaviour in FE or university. Anecdotal evidence suggests an increase in student complaints since the introduction of fees. In the consumer market, goods are measurable against clear criteria, quality statements and/or industry standards. If goods are faulty, a complaint can be made and the goods returned or exchanged. In contrast, students pay for a right of entry onto a programme of study, a service, but may *expect* a right to the qualification or 'the goods'. Thus, education is entering the uneasy world of consumer rights and consumer satisfaction.

Activity 5.1

- As a consumer or buyer of an educational service, identify and rank in order of importance three aspects of an educational service you feel should be included as part of the overall price (expectations). This could include 1:1 support or expectations of teacher knowledge, for example.
- In your groups, take ten minutes to identify and list the impact this might have on student behaviour.
- Select one of these behaviours and identify:
  ◦ one solution to manage the resulting behaviour;
  ◦ one way in which you could have prevented the situation or behaviour from happening.

The continuation and expansion of curriculum range and educational providers remain crucial for both personal development and to meet the needs of the economy, be it through

- further education colleges;
- higher education institutions;

- the voluntary and charitable sector;
- the third and fourth age educational movement;
- the workplace.

The Workers Educational Association (WEA) has, in many ways, been the forerunner of modern adult education. It was established in 1903 with a clear remit to widen access to higher education for the working classes with a focus on quality, standards and improvement. Its aims remain that of 'involving students, volunteers, members and other partners in:

- influencing and campaigning on behalf of adult students;
- removing barriers to learning;
- being responsive in the heart of communities;
- making the most effective use of all our resources;
- promoting learning for life;
- changing and enriching lives through learning – at individual and community levels;
- promoting adult education worldwide.'

Its values include:

- 'creating equality and opportunity, and challenging discrimination;
- believing in people, communities and their potential to change through education;
- putting the learner at the centre of everything we do;
- challenging and questioning ourselves.'

(WEA 2012)

These values denote a different approach to the education of adults to that of traditional pedagogical (child-leading) approaches in which the teacher is viewed as the source of legitimate and credible knowledge, which is then imparted to students. Andragogical (man-leading) approaches, in contrast, are rooted in the humanist school of psychology, described by Malcolm Knowles (1913–97), an American educator, as 'the science and art of helping adults learn' (Knowles 1980).

Theories of adult learning

Traditional approaches argue that children's learning tends to be:

- other-directed;
- inexperienced;
- immature;
- subject-orientated.

Whereas adult learning tends to be:

- self-directed;
- experienced;
- developmental;
- problem-centred (mistakes or problems seen as learning opportunities).

Knowles was the director for the Adult Education Society in America and influenced by the work of psychologist, Carl Rogers (1902–87), philosopher and education reformer, John Dewey (1859–1952), and adult education reformer, Edward Lindeman (1885–1953). Much of his theories of adult students reflect those espoused by Lindeman in *The Meaning of Adult Education* (1926). Both Knowles and Lindeman argue the necessity of alternative educational methods for adults and both advocate that adult learning should:

- develop the self;
- be student- rather than curriculum-led;
- emphasize student learning, rather than teacher 'telling'.

Knowles argued that adults learn through intrinsic motivation, and that they are disposed towards a collaborative and self-directed approach to learning.

❝ By adulthood people are self-directing. This is the concept that lies at the heart of andragogy ... andragogy is therefore student-centred, experience-based, problem-oriented and

> collaborative very much in the spirit of the humanist approach
> to learning and education . . . the whole educational activity
> turns on the student.
>
> *(Burns 1995: 233)* 🙿

While he was not the first to develop an andragogical approach to teaching and learning, his name has become synonymous with this theory. What is not clear is whether this theory was developed as an approach to teaching or as a theory of learning. As a theory of learning Knowles's assumptions about adult students are questionable in a society where a marketized educational system artificially manipulates an instrumentalist approach to learning (Coffield and Williamson 1997). It also fails to recognize pragmatic and strategic approaches to learning favoured by experienced students and those completing work-related courses while working.

The six assumptions of andragogy include:

1 self-concept: self-directing and in control of own learning, ability to choose what, where and how;
2 experience: 'experience is valid knowledge'; adult students are able to bring this knowledge to the classroom to enhance the learning experience;
3 learning ready: open to learning and willing to learn;
4 problem-centred focus: learning more easily assimilated when applied as a solution to real problems;
5 internal motivation: self-esteem, satisfaction, curious and inquiring, an end in itself;
6 a need to know why: adults need to know how new knowledge is useful – the 'meaningfulness' of learning.

Armitage et al. (2003) produced a useful chart comparing the assumptions of andragogy to that of pedagogy (see p. 92).

The assumptions of andragogy can lead to unrealistic expectations about the behaviour of adults. According to Knowles (2005), adult students are more likely to be internally motivated, and consider learning as a means of satisfying curiosity and for self-fulfilment, for example, rather than being driven by external motivators such as qualifications

The assumptions of andragogy		
	Pedagogical	*Andragogical*
Concept of the learner	Dependent personality	Increasingly self-directed
Role of the learner's experience	To be built on more than used as a resource	A rich resource for learning by self and other
Reading to learn	Uniform by age, level and curriculum	Develops from life tasks and problems
Orientation to learning	Subject-centred	Task- or problem-centred
Motivation	By external rewards and punishment	By internal incentives and curiosity

Source: Armitage et al. (2003: 79)

or financial rewards. If, as a teacher, your expectations are of highly motivated students, disengagement can be extremely challenging and difficult to manage. The assumptions of andragogy have implications for the way in which adults are taught and the teaching methods used, which should be designed to make best use of student experiences and existing knowledge, such as discussion. Allowing adult students a voice is essential and for the teacher provides a rich resource which can be utilized. Harnessing such knowledge not only motivates adult students but also can have a profound impact on learner confidence.

Andragogical approaches to teaching can be liberating for both the students and teacher. Paulo Freire, a Brazilian educationalist (1921–97), argued about the need for a co-operative dialogue, and that education revolved around people working with each other rather than to each other. Education can be used to instil conformity and non-questioning acceptance or to liberate the individual through critical questioning and transformation. This emancipatory approach is not new; Francis Bacon (1561–1626), writing in the seventeenth century, despised the external control and prescriptive nature of the curriculum and argued that education should be directed by the learner in a series of observations, exploration and discovery. Originally applied to scientific discovery, Bacon clearly espoused inductive as opposed to deductive learning methods, an approach that was in direct opposition to the didactic instruction favoured at the time.

Inductive teaching methods are inherently more suited to an andragogical teaching style and are rooted in a *humanist* approach. This method allows students to explore and discover principles for themselves. The importance of learning for oneself is described in Charles Kingsley's *The Water Babies* (1863):

> 66 And, if you will read this story nine times over, and then think for yourself, you will find out why. It is not good for little boys to be told everything and never to be forced to use their own wits. They would learn, then, no more than they do at Dr Dulcimer's famous suburban establishment for the idler members of the youthful aristocracy, where the masters learn the lessons and the boys hear them – which saves a great deal of trouble [for the boys] – for the time being. 99

Discovery methods promote understanding, retention and recall as well as maintaining the interest and motivation of students, characteristic of active learning environments, which reduce instances of unwanted behaviour through disengagement, boredom, or the inaccurate pitching of work.

Activity 5.2

Identify a colleague to work with and exchange three lesson plans.
Then conduct an audit of your colleague's lesson plans, and analyse:

- the overall percentage of planned lesson time that is teacher-led. This could include instructions, lectures, explanations and demonstrations, for example, and
- the overall percentage of planned lesson time that actively involves the learner. This could include experiments, problem solving, role play or student debate.

Feed back your findings to your colleague and, in addition, provide one example of how he or she could change a teacher-led activity to one that is student-led.

John Dewey, one of the most influential figures in education over the last century, also firmly rejected the notion of students as passive 'empty vessels' waiting to be filled. Dewey felt that people were shaped by, and in turn shaped, their environments through social interactions. It is therefore the responsibility of adults to promote the learner enquiry and engagement through discovery, experience and hands-on application and problem solving. Crucially, students must be able to relate learning to their own experience and understanding of the world. Regardless of the teaching methods, 'learning ... must always be meaningful and involve active participation and engagement from the learner'.

Discovery methods can be stimulating and engaging, but are also more time-consuming, and some adult students prefer a more strategic approach to learning. Strategic students are those who learn what they need to learn in order to achieve their target in as efficient a manner as possible. A mature student on a Certificate in Education programme described this most eloquently during a group discussion about the importance of learning as an intrinsic good. One member of the group made reference to the proverb 'Give a man a fish and you have fed him for today; teach a man to fish, and you have fed him for a lifetime.' To which this student replied, 'I'm not interested in learning how to fish. I haven't got time to go fishing. I don't want to go fishing. I need to get the kids fed and bathed before the babysitter comes, so I can go to work and, anyway, the only fish they eat comes in finger shapes.' Many adult students are forced to become efficient students in order to successfully juggle work and family commitments with the rigours of learning. Sessions perceived as non-purposeful frequently lead to student challenge, often in a way that is disruptive rather than useful. Experienced practitioners are able to recognize these behaviours and act on them to diffuse the situation, often through making clear the relevance and purpose of the activity. Even if a student does not like, or has no natural interest in, a particular subject, knowing that this will be covered as part of a formal assessment, frequently has a motivating effect.

Research conducted by Marton and Säljö (1976) identified two approaches to learning, that of deep and surface learning. The deep approach involved a holistic view to learning, whereby students read widely about and around a subject to gain a full and deep understanding of the subject and were able to critique and analyse. Surface students adopted a tactical approach that involved uncritical memorizing and recital of key facts or data, often in isolation and only as necessary for the assessment task. Those teachers who are most skilled in the teaching of adults understand the need for an approach to learning that combines the pragmatic approach to surface learning with a need to engage, motivate and enthuse – features of deep and active learning environments.

Alan Rogers (1996: 1) points out that the 'forms and context for teaching adults are many' and it is important to tailor the programme to be taught to both the context and characteristics of the group. In order to avoid misunderstandings, discussions on the structure and purpose of the course with students is crucial to avoid unrealistic expectations from students of the course and of the teacher. This is a two-way process: teachers' expectations of students can be equally unrealistic. Rogers argued for the setting out of a learner/teacher contract and this is a useful way of opening a dialogue with adult students. It is important that teachers encourage openness from students about their learning experience from the start. This can be difficult for adult students who may be used to more traditional teaching methods and who may view constructive feedback as an act of aggression or hostility. As a teacher, you do not have to wait until the end of a course or even the end of a lesson to seek learner feedback or to create opportunities for clarification of purpose and realignment of expectations.

Activity 5.3

- After you have stated the learning objectives of a session, instead of asking students if they understand, ask them what they think these mean. This encourages an open dialogue instead of yes/no responses.
- Use the student responses to clarify expectations and to make the purpose of the session clear.
- At the end of each activity or task, ask the students what they feel they have learned and how useful the activity was for *them* as individuals.
- Analyse the responses: are there any reccurring themes? How high/low were the levels of satisfaction or dissatisfaction? Use ONE aspect of this intelligence to make a change in future practice.

Adult students are among the most motivated of students but their reasons, and thus motivations, for enrolment onto a particular course will differ.

Theories of motivation

Theories of motivation are useful in a number of different settings and for differing purposes. Within business settings, theories of motivation are important in terms of increasing productivity and efficiency. Frederick Taylor's (1856–1915) 'theory of scientific management' (Taylor 1911) claimed that workers are only motivated by pay, do not naturally enjoy work and therefore need close supervision. Work was broken down into small tasks where repetition could improve output and where workers were closely supervised with no autonomy and no input. This theory underpinned Fordist approaches to mass production. Within educational settings, psychological theories of motivation are more frequently rooted in understanding behaviours. 'Motivation' is described as 'an internal state that arouses, directs and maintains behaviour [and] "motivation to learn" as the tendency to find academic activities meaningful and worthwhile and to try and benefit from them' (Woolfolk et al. 2008: 718). There are a number of different theories with regards to motivation, the most common being the difference between **intrinsic motivation** (internal locus of causality) and extrinsic motivation (external locus of causality). When students are intrinsically motivated, they engage in an activity because they want to do so, and not because of what they may achieve or avoid by doing so. Motivation is complex and a variety of factors will influence levels of motivation. Humanists such as Carl Rogers (1902–87) and Abraham Maslow (1908–70) have been of particular significance in adult learning, where learning is seen holistically as a personal striving for growth and fulfilment or 'actualization'. Maslow's hierarchy of needs stresses the importance of intrinsic motivation in learning as extrinsic reasons are not sustainable and once the reward is achieved, there remains no reason to learn. Cognitivists such as Albert Bandura consider self-belief or **self-efficacy** as crucial to student motivation and that those students who believe in their own skills and competence are more likely to achieve.

The planning of sessions that are purposeful, engaging and which focus on a relationship of respect and collaboration are essential for student learning. Incidences of unwanted behaviour occur far less in sessions that are purposeful, well paced, and appropriately differentiated to ensure correct pitch of work. These criteria are essential in all teaching situations and for all levels and age of students. There are, however, some teaching strategies that are particularly effective when teaching adults.

Effective teaching strategies

Increasing learner engagement and interest

Increased engagement correlates to a decrease in unwanted behaviours. You can promote learner interest as follows:

- Ensure learning is meaningful and relevant or has the 'what's in it for me?' factor – be explicit about the purpose of activities and use a range of examples about why a topic is important to match intrinsic or extrinsic motivational factors. An extrinsic example would be making clear there will be an exam question on this topic.
- Ensure lesson plans include a variety of methods and activities that will appeal to a range of learning styles and preferences.
- Make more use of aural and visual resources.
- Plan for active learning environments.
- Talk less and allow students to do more.
- Actively engage the student in the learning process, use a facilitative approach.
- Be open to student feedback to make changes in your teaching style or planning.
- Ensure goals are clear, attainable, and involve a level of challenge to the learner.

Developing a positive rapport

Fostering a climate of trust and developing rapport with adult students are crucial in helping to break down barriers to learning, particularly those associated with low confidence and self-esteem. Invest time in individuals – particularly at the start of the course; this promotes effective rapport and communication. In addition:

- Ensure students are able to speak to you on a 1:1 basis; this is particularly important at the start of courses and at known 'stress' points such as exam or assessment periods.
- Many students will be too embarrassed to say they do not understand a topic or concept in front of their peers. Develop a range of strategies for gathering feedback from students, about your teaching and their learning. One simple method can be to ask students to write down points that require clarification onto Post-it notes, which they can stick to their desks or the wall by the door on their way out.
- Take time to get to know your students and share relevant information about yourself.
- Avoid 'jokey' comments – these often backfire.
- Ensure all feedback is constructive.
- Utilize assessment for learning approaches to encourage dialogue and to ensure students know what they need to know, and you know what students know.
- Treat all students with respect and encourage them to express their views.
- Show you value students by taking an interest in them.
- Reframe statements to build esteem in students and to encourage positive meaning to events or situations.

The skill of **reframing** is an essential part of the educator's toolbox. Reframing is simply changing the meaning of a statement from a negative to a positive. There are two ways of utilizing this in the classroom:

- A learner perspective – to modify actual or perceived levels of learner esteem and confidence. Comments made by teachers can have an impact out of all proportion to that of the intent; this can be particularly true of careless comments. For example, a teacher may feel that he or she is being sympathetic to a student by saying, 'Oh dear, still struggling', and implicitly the teacher may feel this has sent a signal offering help and support. However, the student hears 'You are a failure', and may respond accordingly. This may have a long-lasting effect on the student's self-belief and efficacy. The teacher could have reframed the context by saying, 'I am so impressed by your determination, what an improvement! If you need any help let me know.'

- A teacher perspective – to modify the teacher's view or interpretation of behaviour, that is, the meaning or significance the teacher adds to the actions of others. A verbal challenge, for example, could be interpreted as rude and disruptive. A positive reframing of this behaviour would be to view the verbal challenge as an example of critical thinking and independent thought (a positive). The teacher may need to provide the student with 'nudges' in the right direction, with regard to the most appropriate time for such challenges.

Reframing, like praise, needs to be used appropriately. Overuse can have a negative effect, by reducing the credibility of the 'reframe'.

Activity 5.4

Reframing does not change the situation or the circumstances; it does assign a different meaning which can allow the individual(s) a greater variety of choice and possibilities as to how they will deal with or make sense of the situation. This choice can facilitate positive changes in the attitudes and behaviour of both the teacher and the student. The reframing must be authentic and credible.

Identify one teaching group and either:

- consciously think about your responses to students in terms of their expressed beliefs about their skills and abilities; or
- consciously think about the way you view student behaviours.

Implement reframing techniques over a period of six sessions and then evaluate the impact this has had in the following two areas:

- your views of the group or individuals;
- the views of the students about themselves or their group.

Codify and develop student study skills

Many adult students will come to the classroom with significant knowledge and experience but may not possess the skills needed for effective study, or be clear about the skills required for writing in an academic style, for example. These can act as very powerful barriers to learning and progression as they can have a negative impact on student confidence and self-esteem. As a non-traditional learner, I recall having to look up the 'words' in an essay title to see what they meant, and although I knew what the term 'essay' meant, I had no understanding of how to write an essay. Many adult students will have a spiky profile – high skills in one area but low skill levels in other areas. Poor levels of study skills significantly increase the amount of time it takes to complete a task as students spend time trying to 'find out how' instead of 'doing'. As well as the negative impact on self-esteem this can also reduce levels of motivation and warp notions of how much work is involved in achieving programme outcomes. Many programmes aimed at adult students, particularly non-traditional students, such as Access courses, include a module on study skills.

Activity 5.5

- In small groups produce a list of essential skills, for example, note taking, active reading strategies, or essay plans.
- Identify one which is essential for a particular programme you teach.
- Prepare a 10-minute activity which will develop student understanding and skill in this area.

Study skills are an important element in the teaching of adults. Effective study skills enable adult learners to target their efforts in a much more efficient manner. Many adult students read too widely around a topic, for example, rather than focusing on what is required, and many more procrastinate.

Case study: Cassie

Cassie is a middle manager in a large FE college. Following her recent promotion, Cassie was asked to complete a Level 5 diploma in Management and Leadership. Cassie was halfway through the course when she told her teacher she was thinking of leaving as she could no longer cope with the demands of her job, her family and the programme.

Her teacher asked her to record how many hours she was spending producing an essay. Cassie told her she had spent most evenings and weekends on these. The teacher asked Cassie to record the amount of time actually 'on task'. Cassie found that she was spending only a quarter of the time on task; most of the remaining time was spent fretting about what else she had to do and what she hadn't done.

Following this, Cassie was able to implement a range of strategies to reduce her perceptions about the amount of time she spent on essays. This 'freed' up that wasted time for completion of some of the tasks she had been fretting about. This activity did not decrease the workload or any of Cassie's other commitments, but it did allow Cassie to focus on and develop her time management skills.

Conclusion

Adult students can be complex, straightforward, or a mixture of both. There is no defining characteristic of an adult learner. The reason they participate and enrol on courses is varied, as is their motivation. The diversity and range of students found in adult classrooms, in terms of ability, experience and background, are frequently vast. Differentiation and the ability to tailor sessions according to individual need and aspirations are therefore crucial.

Positive relationships are critical in adult education, as is the ability to communicate in a manner that not only supports learning, but is also able to nurture and allow individuals to achieve their true potential, and **self-actualization**. The importance of adult education as a second chance for improvement and development, be it professional or personal, should not and must not be undermined or devalued: the value of education is worth more than a simple monetary calculation.

Useful website

http://www.stephenbrookfield.com/Dr._Stephen_D._Brookfield/
Workshop_Materials_files/BCRT_Wkshp_Pkt.pdf.
Stephen Brookfield – useful materials and resources to support critical
reflective practice.

References

Armitage, A. *et al.* (2003) *Teaching and Training in Post Compulsory Educa-tion.* Maidenhead: Open University Press.

Armitage, A., Donovan, G., Flanagan, K. and Poma, S. (2011) *Developing Pro-fessional Practice 14–19.* Harlow: Pearson Education.

Biggs, J. (1999) *Teaching for Quality Learning at University.* Buckingham: Open University Press.

BIS (Department for Business Innovation and Skills) (2010) *Further Educa-tion – New Horizon: Investing in Skills for Sustainable Growth.* Avail-able at http://www.bis.gov.uk/assets/biscore/further-education-skills/docs/s/10-1272-strategy-investing-in-skills-for-sustainable-growth.pdf [Accessed 10 January 2012].

Burns, R. (1995) *The Adult Learner at Work.* Sydney: Business and Profes-sional Publishing.

CACE (Central Advisory Council for Education) (England) (1959) *15–18* (Crowther Report). London: HMSO. Available at: http://www.education england.org.uk/documents/crowther/.

CACE (1963) *Half Our Future* (Newsom Report). London: HMSO.

Coffield, F. and Williamson, B. (eds) (1997) *The Repositioning of Higher Edu-cation.* Buckingham: Open University Press.

Committee on Higher Education (1963) *Higher Education* (Robbins Report), Cmnd. 2154. London: HMSO.

Entwhistle, N. (1997) *Styles of Learning and Teaching.* London: David Fulton.

Fox, W.J. (1846) *Lectures: Addressed Chiefly to the Working Classes.* Full text available at: http://www.archive.org/details/lecturesaddresse03foxwiala [Accessed 10 January 2012].

Freire, P. (2007) *Pedagogy of the Oppressed.* New York: Continuum.

HEFCE (Higher Education Funding Council for England) (2010) *Trends in Young Participation in Higher Education: Core Results for England.* Available at http://www.hefce.ac.uk/pubs/hefce/2010/10_03/10_03.doc.

HEFCE (2011) *Diverse Provision in Higher Education: Options and Challenges.* Report to the Department for Business, Innovation and Skills. Available at http://www.hefce.ac.uk/learning/flexible/Diverse_provision.DOC [Accessed 10 January 2012].

Keenan, T. (2002) *An Introduction to Child Development*. London: Sage Publications.

Kingsley, C. (1863) *The Water Babies*. Available at http://www.pagebypage books.com/Charles_Kingsley/The_Water_Babies/.

Knowles, M.S. (1980) *The Modern Practice of Adult Education: From Pedagogy to Andragogy*. Chicago, IL: Follett.

Knowles, M. (2005) *The Adult Learner*, 6th edn. Burlington, MA: Elsevier.

Lindeman, E.C. (1926) *The Meaning of Adult Education*. New York: New Republic.

Marton, F. and Säljö, R. (1976) On qualitative differences in learning: 1 – outcome and process, *British Journal of Educational Psychology*, 46: 4–11.

Merriam, S.B. and Caffarella, R.S. (1991) *Learning in Adulthood*. San Francisco, CA: Jossey-Bass.

Merriam, S.B., Caffarella, R.S. and Baumgartner, L.M. (2007) *Learning in Adulthood: A Comprehensive Guide*, 3rd edn. San Francisco, CA: Jossey-Bass.

National Committee of Inquiry into Higher Education (1997) *Higher Education in the Learning Society* (Dearing Report). London: HMSO.

Petty, G. (2004) *Teaching Today*, 3rd edn. Cheltenham: Nelson Thornes.

Ramsden, P. (1992) *Learning to Teach in Higher Education*. London: Routledge.

Rogers, A. (1996) *Teaching Adults*, 2nd edn. Buckingham: Open University Press.

Rogers, C. (1969) *Freedom to Learn: A View of What Education Might Become*. Columbus, OH: Charles Merrill.

Smith, M.K. (2002) Hannah More: Sunday schools, education and youth work, in *Encyclopaedia of Informal Education*. Available at: http://www.infed.org/thinkers/more.htm [Accessed 10 January 2012].

Smith, M.K. (2004) Adult schools and the making of adult education, in *Encyclopaedia of Informal Education*. Available at: http://www.infed.org/lifelonglearning/adult_schools.htm [Accessed 10 January 2012].

Taylor, F.W. (1911) *The Principles of Scientific Management*. New York: Harper and Row.

UCAS (2011) *End of Cycle Report 2010–11*. Publication Reference 11_237. Available at: http://www.ucas.com/documents/endofcyclereport.pdf [Accessed 10 January 2012].

UCAS (2012) *Data Report 2012. Applicant Figures – November*. Available at: http://www.ucas.com/about_us/media_releases/2011/20111128.

WEA (Workers' Educational Association) (2012) *Aims and Values*. Available at: www.wea.org.uk/about/vision.

Woolfolk, A., Hughes, M. and Walkup, V. (2008) *Psychology in Education*. Harlow: Pearson Education.

CHAPTER

6

A framework for reflection and solution-focused approaches to problems

By the end of the chapter you will be able to:

- apply reflective techniques to improve your own practice;
- understand and apply the *active* use of reflection;
- understand and apply key reflective theories, including those espoused by Schön, Brookfield, Kolb, and Gibbs;
- implement solution-focused approaches to your own practice;
- apply cognitive behavioural approaches in your own practice.

Introduction

Reflection is not a radical or new concept. John Dewey's classic text *How We Think* (1910), for example, has informed the influential theories of both David Boud (Boud et al. 1985) and Donald Schön (1983). 'Reflection' is a generic term that encapsulates a *process* of intellectual consideration and exploration of practice, which professionals undertake in order to improve practice. It plays a significant role in cycles of continuous professional development.

Teachers' attitudes towards reflection vary, as does their systematic use of reflection to improve own or others practice. Many practitioners use reflection on a sporadic basis in reaction to unusual or negative experiences or dilemmas (Tummons 2007). While useful, this is somewhat passive as it limits the practitioner's ability to be proactive and is a model that is dependent on negativity. When used proactively, reflection becomes far more effective, constructive and therefore successful, which in turn increases teachers' confidence, resilience and **self-efficacy**.

This chapter offers a range of reflective strategies and approaches that will develop the practitioner's skill and ability to actively reflect on situations in order to learn from them. Reflection should be honest, objective and solution-focused rather than backward-looking or excessively self-recriminating in nature. Given the number of interactions in any one teaching period, it is not surprising teachers can and do make mistakes, particularly when encountering situations for the first time. *It is the teacher's ability to learn from these mistakes that is both the mark and duty of professionalism and the defining feature of active reflection.*

Self-reflection in isolation is primarily a means of evaluating the performances or behaviours of oneself and others within the teaching and learning environment. *Active* reflection, by definition, requires change. By identifying the solution to the problem, instead of the problem itself, practitioners can refocus their energies on achieving that solution. These types of approaches are most common within the talking therapies of Solution-focused Brief Therapy and Cognitive Behavioural Therapy (CBT).

While teachers are not, and should not, attempt to be psychologists, therapists or counsellors, an understanding and adaptation of solution-focused approaches and cognitive awareness of behaviours can transform reflection from an introspective exercise into a dynamic and vibrant activity. This can over time, enhance and augment the range of personal strategies available to the teacher.

Why use reflective practice?

A core requirement of any professional is the ability to reflect on practice in order to improve practice. It is important to take a 'pick and mix' approach to such theories or frameworks in order to find what works on an individual basis and to ensure reflection becomes meaningful rather than superficial. A framework is a structure or system that supports and allows individuals to make sense of a variety of complex factors.

Key theoretical approaches to reflective practice

There are a number of reflective theories and theorists; two of the most well-known proponents of reflective practice are Donald Schön and Stephen Brookfield. Both Schön's *The Reflective Practitioner* (1983) and Brookfield's *Becoming a Critically Reflective Teacher* (1995) are considered seminal texts. Traditional reflective theories follow the same basic principle: that of learning through experience or, more specifically in this case, learning through reflecting on experience.

This requires the teacher to:

- describe the situation;
- analyse possible causes;
- identify alternatives and strategies for managing the same or similar situation through 'what if' scenarios;
- decide on a new approach – and embed into own practice.

These stages are most clearly reflected in Boud's (Boud et al. 1985) approach, where he invites practitioners:

1 to replay an event and document – and consider what happened; to analyse the event at both cognitive and emotional level;
2 to seek understanding – and identify possible and/or actual reasons;
3 to plan different approaches and responses to enable change.

Kolb (1984) refers to this last point as *active experimentation* and Dewey (1938) as the testing of a *hypothesis* in practice. This testing in practice is critical for developing a continuous cycle of improvement and for developing the teacher's ability to respond to a wider range of classroom situations.

According to Schön, there are two distinct means of reflection within the 'reflective practicum' or learning setting:

- reflection-on-action;
- reflection-in-action.

Reflection-on-action

Reflection-on-action is the *conscious act* of reflecting on a situation or event *after* it has happened, often through replay or documentation. This affords the practitioner the time to explore what happened and, crucially, to consider alternatives, or what might have been 'if'. It is a critical method of reflection, rooted in questioning and enquiry, and promotes an active reflective continuum in the same manner that teacher questions are able to encourage learner critical thinking skills. A progressive approach to learning was endorsed by Dewey in his 1938 text *Experience and Education,* whereby active learning environments were seen as a reaction to traditional passive learning environments.

Critical reflection requires honesty from the practitioner, as well as the skills of detachment and objectivity. Without these skills, practitioners will render themselves closed to different possibilities and new ideas. This is in direct contradiction to the underpinning purpose of reflection, which is to generate new ideas.

Active reflection can therefore be seen as Dewey and Schön intended – a reaction against established patterns and routines.

Reflection-on-action informs and shapes how the practitioner might deal with future situations and is a measured and purposeful act which can be carried out in isolation or with colleagues. One of the important factors about reflection-on-action is that the passage of time between the incident and the reflection often allows practitioners to view a situation more objectively and less emotionally.

Case study

During a teaching session from my own early practice, I recall a male student declaring he would not work with me on a plumbing topic as I was a girl and 'what do girls know?' I responded by asking the pupil to pass me the Polytetrafluoroethylene; when he looked blank, I triumphantly explained that this was the technical name for PTFE tape. At this point, he threw the tape at me and said, 'As you're so bloody clever, you can do it yourself.'

When reflecting on this situation later and to colleagues I was at first defensive and tried to justify my actions. Although on the surface this incident had been resolved, I continued to worry about the incident for many weeks afterwards, often through replaying the situation. I went through a variety of feelings at differing stages of this process. It was not until I accepted my role in triggering the event that I was able to learn from this and move forward in a positive and proactive way.

Reflection-in-action

Reflection-in-action is frequently described as 'thinking on your feet'. While often reactive, reflection-in-action draws on the previous experiences and learning of the teacher and, crucially, is the point at which this learning is applied in practice. To be able to think about the consequences of actions, either your own or that of the learner, while experiencing the situation, sounds complicated but is often made more simple though experience of similar situations, and 'knowing'. Schön links 'knowing' with the theory of tacit knowledge. This is knowledge that is ingrained to such a degree that we do not have to think about it, so that it is done automatically. While such tacit knowledge is useful, it can become habitualized behaviour and thus unchallenged by the practitioner. It is only through challenge that practitioners are able to expand their horizons and thus the possibility of innovation. Without challenge, ideas become assumptions, assumptions beliefs, and beliefs 'facts'.

Mental or cognitive frameworks or **schema** are ways in which humans are able to interpret and understand complicated data and information. Schema are developed over time and rooted in experience. They often provide a short cut to the understanding or rationalizing of behaviours for the practitioner. Understanding behaviour is important when dealing with a situation as it unfolds, as an understanding of the behaviour and reasons behind behaviour influences the teacher's responses to that behaviour.

Schemas can be adapted and modified, which in turn create new knowledge and understanding. Practitioners are able to add these to their own personal toolkit of strategies. Challenges to accepted 'knowing' can be difficult to recognize and in some cases practitioners will add meaning which only serves to enforce their current beliefs, rather than changing, adapting or modifying personal schema. Entrenched schema are difficult to challenge, especially when practitioners see no reason to change (they are after all 'right'). Self-reflection in these situations only enforces those beliefs.

Critical reflection and challenge allow the practitioner to explore the match or congruence between belief and reality.

Argyris and Schön (1974) referred to this as the difference between 'espoused theory' and that of 'theory in use'. Many practitioners, for example, say they are inclusive but sometimes their actions are not. It often takes an outside perspective to examine and explore underpinning values in order to expose any lack of congruence.

Although teaching is itself an isolating experience, the sharing of that experience does not have to be. Sharing experiences with trusted and non-judgemental colleagues allows others to challenge and question our own behaviours. It is for this reason that open and trusting cultures are so important in any organization, particularly so within educational settings. Argyris and Schön suggest questioning one's own values and ideologies and then deliberately acting as if they are wrong often leads to new ideas and practice. Lessons learned from this approach support professional development in a way that is far more effective, as they are meaningful to the teacher.

Stephen Brookfield also developed theories of reflective practice and in particular critical reflection. Like Argyris and Schön, he argues the need for practitioners to question personal and wider social or cultural assumptions. The following is a useful starting point when trying to develop critical thinking skill sets. For Brookfield, the critical thinking process requires the following stages:

1 identify assumptions;
2 check accuracy and validity;
3 take alternative perspectives;
4 take informed actions.

(Brookfield 2006)

In order to identify assumptions we may need to seek alternative views. Assumptions are often so deep-rooted we are not aware of them and rarely codify or explicitly espouse them. For this reason, it is often easier to identify assumptions in others and, conversely, it is easier for others to identify these assumptions within ourselves.

In order to improve professional practice, teachers need to gather evidence about their teaching. Analysis of such information and data allows the practitioner to identify areas of good practice and those areas requiring improvement. For Brookfield, information is gathered through four key portals or 'lenses':

- autobiographical lens (how we view ourselves as teachers);
- through the eyes of our colleagues;
- through the eyes of our students;
- through the literature and theory.

Autobiographical lens

By viewing teaching through these differing lenses, teachers are able to get different perspectives on themselves as teachers and on their teaching skills. Examination of own learning and experiences enables teachers to identify areas of good practice and those areas which need development. During the initial stages of teacher training programmes, a common exercise is to ask the trainees to reflect on their own experiences of being taught – the good, the bad and the painful. Many trainees root their teaching persona or 'teacher identity' on those experiences.

Colleagues

The second lens is through colleagues. Information can be gathered through formal means such as observation or through less formal approaches such as discussions. Peer observations are a powerful development tool as long as this process is engaged in openly, in a developmental and transparent way. Observations can feel exposing and require a significant amount of trust. Although, peer observations are significantly less threatening when teachers are feeling confident, it is worth remembering that the simple confirmation of existing skills will offer few developmental opportunities. Where confidence is lacking, particularly with less experienced teachers or those teachers experiencing challenging groups, it is often better to build a rapport and jointly develop ideas for the lesson before the observation is scheduled. In isolation, a teacher is one person. Through discussion, collaboration and sharing of practice they can benefit from the experiences of many.

The culture of an organization or department is crucially important in developing open and transparent trusting cultures. These are cultures where staff are encouraged to explore their own practice in order to improve it and where staff do not feel they will be disadvantaged or criticized.

> 66 It requires a moral and political culture characterized by openness to diverse perspectives and ideologies, and a respectful acknowledgement of the importance of each person's contribution, irrespective of seniority or status. Creating this culture involves breaking patterns that emphasize competitiveness and a privatization of knowledge.
>
> *(Brookfield 1995)* 99

Students

The third lens is through the eyes of the students. It is important to gauge feedback from students in order to determine:

- student understanding;
- information about the way in which the teacher communicates;
- efficacy of teaching and impact on learning.

Changes made following learner feedback often have the most direct impact on students and their learning.

Communication is an essential element of all teaching and learning and is the mechanism through which teachers convey overt and covert information. Miscommunication is frequently a key factor in challenging behaviour. The messages teachers intend to convey are not always the messages received by the student. Feedback questionnaires can be utilized to check learner experience and adaptions implemented as required. Students will have differing learning preferences and attitudes towards learning. Those attitudes may change over time and are especially sensitive to external influences, it is therefore important to change teacher approaches to accomodate these changes in learners behaviours.

Brookfield also developed the use of the critical incident questionnaire to seek formal feedback from students, and a variety of models exist. These can be developed to suit group needs or to gain specific information.

Activity 6.1

Ask your students these four questions, only one item issue per question:

- What did you like the most?
- What surprised you?
- What did you like the least?
- What would you change?

You can record student responses in a variety of ways to suit your purpose. Post-it notes or 'show me' wipe boards encourage quick, brief, one-word answers. This allows the practitioner to find out what went well or otherwise, but not necessarily why. Further research and reflection are then required. Many practitioners engage in more formal or systematic methods of reflection after a challenging event has occurred. It is just important to reflect on sessions that have gone well in order to replicate and build on 'good' sessions.

Literature and theory

The final lens is through that of the theoretical literature. This lens is useful for developing ideas and making sense of our experiences. The ability to apply or name theories and relate them to our own practice can be an affirming process. It is also useful for maintaining perspective and is an important additional source of information other than that of experience.

Although reflection through a particular lens is in itself useful, combining all four will allow the practitioner to gain insight into the 'whole' situation. The ability to scrutinize assumptions and values is integral to a number of theories of critical reflection. Experience without reflection can lead to stagnation. For Brookfield, critical reflection is a liberating activity: 'Not to be reflective is to live in the present as a prisoner of the past' (1995: 265).

Activity 6.2

This exercise requires three people:

- The *storyteller* (teacher/actor) recounts an experience of challenging behaviour and how he or she dealt with it.
- The second person acts as *detective* trying to gather more information, and deliberately seeks 'flaws' in the evidence.
- The third person is the *observer* and his/her role is to observe responses and note any assumptions or judgements.

Part 1

At the end of the 'story' all feed back their views of the situation and identify

- differences;
- similarities.

Part 2

Actions

- In isolation, identify one way in which you will plan to do things differently.

Share this with your colleagues

- Adapt and improve your response following their constructive advice.

Brookfield (2006)

Other influential theorists

David Kolb's (1984) influential experiential learning cycle is used extensively within the field of reflective practice. For Kolb, the reflective cycle can start at any stage as long as it is followed in sequence and cyclically. The core elements replicate those found in Dewey's, Schön's and Brookfield's theories:

- the experience;
- reflecting on the experience;
- securing further insight through additional sources such as the literature (abstract conceptualization);
- trying out or testing of that new knowledge within practice.

This model is simple to apply and its common-sense learning from experience approach appeals to both new and experienced practitioners.

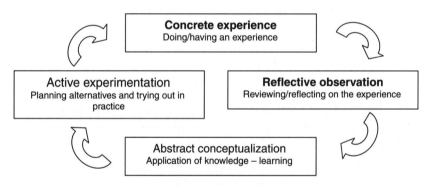

Graham Gibbs further developed this model in 1988 and, crucially, included feelings. This method allows the practitioner to consider each phase and aspect of a situation when reflecting. It is active and able to ask critical questions of the practitioner. The evaluation stage offers the practitioner the chance to identify good practice as well as areas for improvement and the conclusion and action plan allow the opportunity for redemption. Reflection should not be used as a tool for self-recrimination; while acknowledgement of mistakes is important in order to learn from those mistakes, rectifying mistakes embodies the practitioner's continued development in and capacity to learn from practice in order to change practice.

Source: http://www.brookes.ac.uk/services/upgrade/a-z/reflective_gibbs.html

The recognition of personal feelings is essential to authentic reflection: when things go badly it makes us feel bad and, conversely, when things go well we feel good. Feelings impact on practice, negative experiences can lead to a reduction in confidence and also a reluctance to try new or different approaches, particularly those which involve risk. Some of these feelings can be internalized and may require significant time, through self-reflection and discussions with trusted colleagues, before confidence is regained.

Authentic reflections about such incidents will lead to resolution and acceptance of our own mistakes. It is important to remember that while honest reflection does not justify or excuse behaviours or choices, it can often explain them. This allows us to learn more about who we are and why we behave in the way we do. **Active reflection** becomes a learning activity.

One of the most useful models to utilize when considering emotions is that of Batari's Box. This is a simple reflective model that focuses on the teacher's emotional state or attitude.

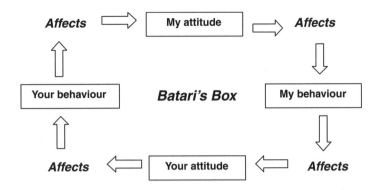

Jodi Roffey-Barentsen and Richard Malthouse (2009) provide a simple example of the impact teachers' emotions have on their professional practice. They describe a teacher who is running late for a meeting when a student stops and asks her for advice on an assignment. It is the third time the teacher has been stopped on the way to this meeting and she has already provided the student with support about the assignment. In exasperation, she tells the student she has already helped him and if he listens to her advice, he will be okay. This has a negative impact on the student who only 'sees' rejection, and his perception is of a teacher that, when asked for help, 'can't be bothered'.

Activity 6.3

- List three possible consequences as a result of this negative interaction.
- List three actions the teacher could have planned and implemented which would have avoided this situation, for example, scheduled drop-in sessions for student support (pre-emptive planned action).
- List one way in which you would act differently if the situation reoccurred, for example, explain why you can't help now, but could at a later time (planned alternative reaction).

Moving from reflection to action

The previous models utilize reflection upon the experience or the past as the first step towards action. Focusing on the future and the changes required to effect ideal futures can be an extremely effective alternative approach, as it directly influences the agent of change. In addition, if as teachers we accept that we can never fully understand or know why events occur or not, or when they will be repeated, reflection in isolation is in danger of becoming rumination or brooding. This can decrease teacher optimism or proactive responses, lending itself instead to self-blame and excuses. While some practitioners will plan for changes, some will make minor adaptations, but without any significant change, and many more intend to make changes but will not actually implement any changes. 'One of the hardest things teachers have to learn is that the sincerity of their intentions does not guarantee the purity of their practice' (Brookfield 1995: 1).

Solution-focused brief approaches

Solution-focused brief approaches begin by defining the intended or preferred outcome. Thus, causes of behaviour are acknowledged but action is even more important than consideration of causes, which can be misleading or serve as distraction or procrastination! In addition, there are many cases where the causes or reasons for the event or behaviour are unknown. When this happens, reflectors often find themselves repeatedly going over the event or behaviour and so become enmeshed in a continuous and often negative cycle of 'why'. By focusing on preferred outcomes instead of reasons, the teacher is able to move forward and, while the event is acknowledged, the focus is on identifying the possibilities of alternative pathways for the present and the future, as opposed to being rooted or 'stuck' in the past.

Solution-focused brief approaches work by supporting individuals to recognize and focus on the positive – what has gone well and previous successes, thus embedding a 'can do' approach which is critical for building self-confidence particularly in terms of own efficacy.

When faced with a problem, a solution-focused approach requires the teacher to:

- imagine a world in which a 'miracle has occurred overnight' (problem disappears);

- be able to describe this ideal world (targets or goals);
- describe how they would know a miracle had happened (what would be different – list the improvements).

Solution-focused brief therapy was developed and refined within a therapeutic mental health setting in the United States. The two key proponents were Steve de Shazer (1940–2005), and Insoo Kim Berg (1934–2007). Since this time the approach, with its emphasis on the present and future and on solutions, has been adapted in a variety of settings. The focus is on clarity of goal setting and how to achieve change. It relies on the individual to imagine and effect this change, an empowering approach that validates the practitioner's ability to make positive change and therefore improvements. As indicated by its name, solution-focused brief approaches are fast acting and immediate.

The solution-focused brief approach provides the practitioner with the tools to change dynamics within the classroom both during and after the session. As with many effective strategies, it is simple but requires practice in order to allow the teacher to feel comfortable with its use. It goes beyond simplistic positive outlooks through the mutual engagement of the teacher and learner. For example, instead of simply saying 'congratulations' to students, teachers asks *how* they achieved success. This ensures that students are able to recognize and rehearse their own role in achievement and thus develop their own capacity to repeat and build on this success. It is similar to constructive feedback whereby the marker will note exceptions, good and bad, and why these worked or otherwise. The crucial difference, however, is that the dialogue is based not on teacher telling, but teacher asking and student telling.

A solution-focused approach in the classroom is led and shaped by the teacher; it is a positive outlook that can be learned. This is difficult at first and will feel like acting to start with, but with time and practice, it becomes who you are. This positive approach must remain authentic and meaningful; solution-focused practitioners must recognize the reality of the difficulties faced as opposed to avoiding, ignoring or trivializing them.

Recognition of daily pressures is important when reflecting and workload pressures can often mean a teaching day is something to get through, an endurance test, rather than something to be shared and enjoyed. Webb (1999) sees this as a problem-focused approach to teaching, rather than a solution-focused approach. This can be illustrated in the following table:

Problem-focused	Solution-focused
Excuses	Exceptions
Fixing	Creating
Stuck	Forward-moving
Deficits and needs	Abilities and resources
Failures	Successes
Blaming	Partnering
What is *not* working	What *is* working
Past	Present and future
What's wrong	What's right
Problem	Purpose
Control	Responsibility

Source: Webb (1999)

It is easy to see that the first column roots the practitioner in the past, while the second column is forward-looking and open to a range of possibilities. Consider the excuses we all make and hear on a daily basis, whether in reference to the 'graveyard' slot on a Friday afternoon, or 'What do you expect after the Christmas holidays?' to 'He has ADHD. . .'. Developing awareness of these 'excuses' and presenting them as exceptions rather than constants paves the way for new and different alternatives. Grading these issues helps to identify those areas of practice that need immediate attention and scaling enables the practitioner to identify and implement the bite-sized changes to make immediate improvement.

There are 5 stages to this approach:

- *Stage 1*: the problem recognized
  Dialogue begins – problem codified and 'made real', honesty and openness rather than denial and blame.
- *Stage 2*: The miracle question
  What would your life be like without the problem? If this miracle happened overnight, how would you know the miracle had

occurred? Describe the post-miracle differences that would evidence the change.

- *Stage 3*: solution building
Exceptions – when was the problem less of a problem? When did you manage it better, for example, when was the last time you did not get angry in the same situation? If you did not get angry, what impact would this have? What would the difference be?

  This allows you to see the problems as an exception and also identify times when you have managed the problems – thus you can identify alternative solutions which draw on your own experience of success

- *Stage 4*: scaling
Scaling a problem helps to put the problem or problems in context and supports solution building by allowing you to identify those small but significant improvement steps.

  A problem is graded between 1 and 10 where 1 is the worst case scenario and 10 the best case scenario.

Worst case scenario   **Best case scenario**

1   10

You need to identify what would have to happen to improve a situation from its current grade, for example 4, to the next grade – a 5. In this way, you can monitor and track your own progress. It also allows you to identify problems that require immediate attention and those which can be addressed at a later point in time.

- *Stage 5*: termination – this issue has been dealt with and finished.

Case study

Consider the following scenario: an adult learner expresses her view, which the teacher disagrees with. The teacher tells the learner she is wrong. The learner walks out of the session.

Scenario	Problem-focused	Consequences
Learner expresses a view	Teacher tells her she is wrong	Student feels bad No opportunity to discuss Monologue – teacher-led Teacher controlling Learner walks out of session Teacher blames the student Student blames the teacher

When asked to reflect on this incident, the teacher explains that it is an adult education session and adult students should be open to challenge and questioning. It is the duty of the practitioner to ensure this happens, and if the student is not open to this type of challenge, then perhaps she should not be on the programme.

This response illustrates the teacher's embedded assumption about the nature of adult students. It is also defensive and focuses on blame and the problem. The teacher is invited to explore alternatives to this approach and, because they are couched in terms of 'what ifs', the problem is able to be externalized, rather than internalized. The teacher is asked to describe situations where challenge occurred and where a student did not walk out – exceptions. The teacher is able to do this and is complimented on these successful approaches.

The teacher is asked to imagine an ideal scenario where challenge occured, but which led to different and more positive outcomes the iden-tification of the differences that would occur.

Scenario	Solution-focused	Consequences
Learner expresses a view	Teacher asks them to imagine exceptions to this assertion and 'what ifs'	Two-way dialogue Facilitation Partnership Creativity Alternatives

The consequences of the *solution-focused* approach compared with the *problem-focused* approach are as follows:

- learner remains in session and is engaged and part of the learning process;
- teacher facilitates a questioning approach and embeds critical enquiry into learning and teaching experience;
- student may or may not agree, but is willing to explore alternatives.

The simplicity of solution-focused brief approaches allows the person to focus on alternative futures rather than perceived failures of themselves, or others, or the past.

The table below is useful to support identification of the differences between a problem-focused and a solution-focused approach.

Practitioner approach	Attitudes	Consequences
Problem-focused	Student's fault if she is not able to listen (excuses) Teachers should tell students when they are wrong (assumes the teacher is 'expert' – traditional pedagogical approach) *Focus on what is wrong*	No change Teacher needs to exert more power to retain control Students increasingly passive
Solution-focused	Teacher reflects on future alternatives and identifies model solution Teacher plans and implements steps to model solution Teacher takes responsibility for students' learning *Focus on what can be done differently*	Change Teacher exerts less power and more influence Learning is a facilitated two-way process Students increasingly responsible for own learning and active in this process

The consequences for the learner of a *problem-focused* attitude are as follows:

- learning is passive and sole responsibility of the teacher or 'expert', not the student;
- student learns failure and blame (teacher is rubbish);
- the student develops a 'can and won't do' approach to learning.

A *solution-focused* attitude, on the other hand, results in the following consequences. The learner:

- assumes responsibility for own learning;
- assumes credit for successes;
- develops increased self-esteem;
- is able to learn from mistakes and view these as exceptions;
- develops a 'can do' approach to learning.

Activity 6.4

Use the table on p. 125 to:

- identify one area of your teaching you would like to be different;
- identify the 'now' – what it is about this situation or issue that is distressing or frustrating;
- envisage how it could be different – ask yourself the miracle question;
- identify and apply the miracle cure: 'What would this situation look like in the ideal world?';
- if no one told you the miracle had occurred, how would you know it had happened – what would be different? Identify the differences in terms of what the student would be doing differently and what you would be doing differently.

The table illustrates the focus of this activity, which is to identify the 'ideal outcome', and how you would 'know' this had happened. As stated, it is often easier for the teacher to focus on the negative rather than the positive. Therefore the ability to recognize positives

Current situation	Consequences	Miracle cure ideal situation	Differences on learning and teaching
	What are the effects for learning and teaching?		How would you know the miracle cure had happened?
Describe Objectively what is happening No blame or cause seeking	Consider the impact on the learning of the student Consider the impact on teaching	What you would like to happen Ideal solution	Before After

is an important attitudinal shift towards solution-focused rather than problem-based practice. The briefness and goal-orientated core of solution-focused brief approaches allow the teacher to apply such techniques 'in situ'. It forms a mode of communication that does not require the development of therapeutic-type relationships, which need to be developed over time, but can be used instantaneously.

Using scaling to plan the changes

Scaling questions enable the practitioner to plan the journey towards the best outcome. Many teachers will recognize the need to break learning down into manageable chunks yet do not apply such techniques to their own development. Indeed, many teachers report that part of being a teacher is the need to portray themselves as 'all knowing', without which they lose credibility and authority. This needs to display their own knowledge and skill is often associated with staff who are newly qualified or who have experienced difficulties. It is often a feature of lack of confidence and lack of belief in one's ability to effect change or self-efficacy. The very nature of teaching is, of course, exposing and, as one trainee remarked: 'If you put your head above the parapet, you are bound to get hit at some point.'

Solution-focused brief approaches are by nature optimistic, and reduce opportunities for disagreement – the focus is on 'ideal futures', not previous wrongdoing, or perceived wrongdoing, blame or failure. Scaling starts at zero or 1 for the worst-case scenario through to 10 as the best-case scenario. Often the situation is such that the student or teacher feels the situation to be hopeless – hence the use of the miracle cure question, which acknowledges the possibility of change. In these situations, scaling allows the practitioner to identify the steps needed to make an immediate improvement. It is amazing what is possible when one clear and achievable goal is required, as opposed to perfection!

Scaling questions are used to identify a point on a scale. This allows two types of questions to follow:

1 'Coping' questions: for example, 'Given the difficulties, you are coping extremely well. You are at 4 and not 3. What is it that you are doing to stop things becoming worse?' This supports resilience, through acknowledgement of those strengths.
2 'Instead of' questions: it is easy to say what shouldn't happen, but rarely do we identify what we should do instead. This is important as it allows the person to explore alternatives, to experiment and identify the solutions needed.

Once a point on a scale is identified, the next stage is to categorize one small change that would move the point onwards. Scales can be used multiple times and in multiple aspects.

Self-reflecting can be difficult and teachers may need to develop a range of strategies to support this. The use of the empty chair technique, a Gestalt role play tool for developing self-awareness and self-responsibility, can help support the establishment of a dialogue where 'one part of you' is the questioner and the 'other part of you' the respondent.

The purpose of the questioning is to identify the ideal outcome or goal and to develop participants' understanding of their own skills and strengths in terms of exceptions. Recognition of exceptions enables the teacher to realize that things can be done differently and, crucially, that he or she already has many of the answers, solutions and skills to avoid or manage problems as evidenced by exceptions. This approach acknowledges the difficulties of the problems faced by the teacher while also validating the positive actions taken which have led to solutions in other situations. Strengths and successes are emphasized instead of deficits and weaknesses. This increases confidence and feelings of self-efficacy, promoting resilience instead of helplessness.

Teachers can apply solution-focused brief approaches as one of many tools within their own self-reflection armoury. They can also be used within teaching practice to change the behaviours and attitudes of learners. When done successfully this allows students to become partners in the learning process.

This introduction to the positive aspects of solution-focused brief approaches is not intended to be, or to replace, professional therapy. Utilization of such strategies, with a focus on identifying the changes needed to improve practice will lead to improved teaching and learning.

In some cases, it is not the problem but meaning individuals assign to the 'problem' or situation. For example, a friend invites you to a large party. Do you feel:

- excited – all those new people to dazzle and charm;
- nonchalant – you would rather be on the settee with a glass of wine, your favourite blanket and a good film;
- apprehensive – you know you'll be left alone in the corner, you always say the wrong thing and to top it all you are bound to get the dress code wrong.

In the above example, it is clear from the first two responses that the party itself is not a problem. This is not the case for the third response. Cognitive Behavioural Therapy (CBT) supports individuals to recognize the impact of individual thoughts (cognitions) on behaviour. Understanding some of the techniques used in such therapies can have a profound impact on our thoughts and, behaviours including our teaching behaviours.

Cognitive behavioural approaches

Cognitive behavioural approaches are similar to solution-focused brief approaches in that they too are rooted in the present rather than the past. This necessitates a problem-solving approach and use of own skills and attributes to embed long-term changes and improvements. Like solution-focused brief therapy, cognitive behavioural therapy (CBT) has had considerable success, particularly in the treatment of anxiety disorders. A primary focus is to modify or adapt behaviours and break negative patterns of behaviour, often associated with distorted thinking or perceptions.

When dealing with difficult groups or individuals it is often our own thought processes and the meaning we attach to events that can lead to feelings of low esteem, reduced confidence and guilt and thus reduced perceptions of self-efficacy. These are often inaccurate and unhealthy. They can also increase the intensity of the problem.

Using the same scenario as before, in which a learner walks out of a session, the table below illustrates two different approaches to the event.

	Unhealthy	*Healthy*
Practitioner approach	It's my fault I'm a rubbish teacher. I should never have challenged that student; in fact, it wasn't a challenge. It was just rude and me trying to exert power over that student Not only am I a rubbish teacher, I am a rubbish human being	I handled that badly I could have handled things differently I will do 'x' differently next time I made a mistake and I will rectify it
Conclusion drawn	I am a bad teacher (and a bad person)	That was a bad strategy
Emotion	Guilt	Remorse

(Continued)

	Unhealthy	*Healthy*
Consequences	Original event escalated out of proportion Negative feelings increase Blame Confidence and self-worth decrease Not useful for teacher or student	Event acknowledged Responsibility and role in event acknowledged Healthy reflection and analysis of the event Plans different responses Remorse leads to restorative action Positive feelings associated with restorative action increase self-confidence, esteem and efficacy
Resulting impact on teacher	**Internalization of 'problem' (me)** **Reduced ability (without challenge) to perceive pathways for change** **'Self-downing'**	**Externalization of event** **Easier to envisage alternatives** **'Self-acceptance'**

'Self-downing' refers to excessive self-criticism. 'Self-acceptance', in contrast, is a healthier and more realistic response, especially as teachers can and will continue to make mistakes.

The following list indicates a range of unhealthy responses when engaged in constantly or over a prolonged period of time. These include:

- Self-destructive behaviours:
  - excessive drinking;
  - illegal drug taking or abuse of legal or prescriptive drugs;
  - over-/under-eating.
- Mood-lowering behaviours:
  - self-isolating;
  - over-sleeping;
  - staying indoors.

- Avoidance behaviours:
  - not answering the phone;
  - avoiding threatening situations;
  - putting off tasks.

Adapted from Branch and Wilson (2007: 16)

These behaviours can enforce or exacerbate existing feelings of inadequacy or feelings such as despair. This in turn impacts on behaviours, thoughts and personal beliefs, creating a negative spiral which can be difficult to change.

Challenging own thoughts is similar to Schön's 'critical reflection' and Brookfield's 'confrontation of assumptions'. This is also known as 'cognitive restructuring'. It requires the person to identify the negative thoughts, to analyse the distorted aspects of these beliefs and to replace them with thoughts that are more realistic. Solution-focused brief approaches can support the later stages of this process as can discussing events with colleagues and friends to identify different, and perhaps more realistic, views or interpretations of the event.

The following chart is a frequently used tool to support identification of unhealthy or problematic thoughts and behaviours and is commonly referred to as the 'ABC' method.

A (activating event)	B (belief, thought)	C (emotional and behavioural consequences)
Student walks out of session	I am a bad teacher I failed	Emotional: guilt, anxiety Behavioural: defensive, hostile, problem-focused, avoidance of same or similar situations No change in behaviour or thoughts

The above examples illustrate the ease with which individuals can slip into **catastrophizing**, or, 'making mountains out of molehills' (Branch and Wilson 2007). This is where an event is believed to have far more serious consequences than it actually has.

Activity 6.5

Think of an example from your own practice where you made a mistake or, if possible, identify a situation which (given time, reflection and perhaps a little challenge) you can see you may have got things a little out of perspective!

1 Write down a minimum of six *exaggerated* responses to the event and then using the ABC chart sort these into beliefs and emotional and behavioural consequences.

   For example, using the scenario above, where a student walks out of a session:
   • It is all my fault
   • I should not have told him he was wrong
   • I am the worst teacher
   • I make their lives worse not better
   • He will never come back to this classroom again
   • Now everyone knows how crap I am . . .

2 Now use a series of challenge questions to encourage a healthier interpretation of the event:
   • 'True/false' statements: was it all your fault? Should you have let his view go unchallenged?
   • What evidence is there to support or dispute these claims?
   • Would a colleague come to the same conclusion – why/why not?

3 Then step into the role of 'Pollyanna' and play the 'glad game'. This is where, no matter how bad or extreme the situation appears, you must find the positives. Thus, walking out of the room allowed the student the space and time to calm down and provided an unplanned learning opportunity for the teacher . . .

Polarizing events like this are useful in helping the teacher to recognize unhealthy feelings and identify or assign meanings that are healthier and more productive emotional and behavioural responses.

Constantly worrying about an event will not reduce the likelihood of the event happening, but will increase anxiety levels. Avoidance is a common strategy but often leads to escalation of the problem. A refusal to open bills, for example, does not reduce debt.

Confronting and dealing with unhelpful behaviours in oneself and others is an important process in becoming resilient and developing coping strategies. Recognition of problematic beliefs and behaviours is often the first step in addressing and changing such beliefs and behaviours. In order to achieve change, clarity of goals is essential. A useful strategy is the production of a 'pros' and 'cons' list, whereby the benefits or cost of staying the same, are compared to the cost of change.

For example, a student who is avoiding writing an essay, because they have a fear of failing, will fail if he or she does not submit. In addition, the long-term impact could further enforce an already negative view of the self and develop a 'can't do' attitude. By weighing up the costs of change, as shown in the table, individuals are able to evaluate choices in a more realistic manner.

Action	Cost advantages	Cost disadvantages
Short-term Work on essay	Possibility of success – I might pass	Time
Medium-term Submit essay	Sense of achievement and of changing unhelpful behaviours and beliefs	Risk of failure – but now only a risk not a definite
Long-term Essay fails	May feel better for *trying* Will have received constructive feedback and advice to support a future pass Development of healthy coping strategies and resilience Could mean greater long term ending power increase in self-esteem Will develop confidence and	Reinforces distorted view about the self Position becomes entrenched No worse than current position if I do fail
Essay passes	self-belief Will support development of a 'give it a go' approach Sense of pride in achievement	

This approach may seem simplistic but cost, be it financial or emotional, can be a highly motivating factor when considering change.

Conclusion

This chapter offers you a range of approaches to enable critical reflection, as well as a range of strategies to effect change and improve on your practice. In order to be effective, reflection is dependent upon honesty and authenticity. This involves difficult and sometimes extremely challenging critical questions of the self and others.

In essence, traditional reflective theories rely on

- understanding: the situation;
- analysing: what happened, why, what you could have done differently, what you would do differently next time;
- agency – to act or implement change.

For many, reflective practice is a way of life used to reflect on both the unusual or exceptional as well as the routine. For others, reflection can be used as a cathartic process in the journey of 'coming to terms' with a particular situation. Reflection, both 'in' and 'on' practice, allows the practitioner to develop a range of planned strategies and responses to similar experiences. Active solution building and change enable the practitioner to utilize and recognize existing strengths and skills, thereby increasing confidence, resilience and efficacy. Critical reflection also supports professional integrity and enables practitioners to interrogate and scrutinize their own teaching, values and behaviours. There are occasions, when teachers react badly and sometimes they teach badly. Alexander Pope, an English poet, wrote 'To err is human, to forgive, divine.' Self-forgiveness is important when facing the truth, but even more important is the ability to learn from our mistakes. To teach is to encounter new situations every day. This is what makes teaching so exciting and also a little risky. Enjoy all experiences and view each session as an opportunity for learning and self-development.

Useful websites

http://www.bbc.co.uk/science/leonardo/thinker_quiz/research.shtml
BBC Science website - what kind of a thinker are you?

http://www.stephenbrookfield.com/Dr._Stephen_D._Brookfield/Critical_Incident_Questionnaire.html
Stephen Brookfield – Critical Incident Questionnaires

http://www.stephenbrookfield.com/Dr._Stephen_D._Brookfield/Workshop_Materials_files/Critical_Thinking_materials.pdf
Stephen Brookfield – Developing critical thinkers: additional materials. A range of scenarios and additional materials to support the development of critical thinking.

http://www.ofsted.gov.uk/
Ofsted – the Office for Standards in Education, Children's Services and Skills: the body which regulates and inspects these services and by which all educational provision is judged.

http://www.parliament.uk
Contains particularly useful links which allow members of the public to view progress on proposed Bills.

References

Argyris, C. and Schön, D. (1974) *Theory in Practice*. San Francisco, CA: Jossey-Bass.

Boud, D., Keogh, R. and Walker, D. (1985) *Reflection: Turning Experience into Learning*. London: Kogan Page.

Branch, R. and Wilson, R. (2007) *Cognitive Behavioural Workbook for Dummies*. Chichester: John Wiley and Sons Ltd.

Brookfield, S.D. (1995) *Becoming a Critically Reflective Teacher*. San Francisco, CA: Jossey-Bass.

Brookfield, S.D. (2006) *Developing Critical Thinkers*. Available at: http://www.stephenbrookfield.com/Dr._Stephen_D._Brookfield/Workshop_Materials_files/Critical_Thinking_materials.pdf.

Department for Education (2010a) *The Case for Change*. Available at: http://www.education.gov.uk/publications/standard/publicationDetail/Page1/DFE-00564-2010.

Department for Education (2010b) *The Importance of Teaching* (White Paper). Available at: https://www.education.gov.uk/publications/standard/publicationdetail/page1/CM%207980.

Dewey, J. (1910) *How We Think*. Lexington, MA: D. C. Heath.

Dewey, J. (1938) *Experience and Education*. New York: Macmillan.

Gibbs, G. (1988) *Learning by Doing: A Guide to Teaching and Learning Methods*. Oxford: Further Education Unit, Oxford Polytechnic.

Johns, C. (2000) *Becoming a Reflective Practitioner*. Oxford: Blackwell.

Kolb, D. (1984) *Experiential Learning*. Englewood Cliffs, NJ: Prentice Hall.

Roffey-Barentsen, J. and Malthouse, R. (2009) *Reflective Practice in the Lifelong Learning Sector*. Exeter: Learning Matters.

Schön, D. (1983) *The Reflective Practitioner*. New York: Basic Books.

Schön D. (1987) *Educating the Reflective Practitioner*. San Francisco, CA: Jossey-Bass.

Tummons, J. (2007) *Becoming a Professional Tutor in the Lifelong Learning Sector*. Exeter: Learning Matters.

Webb, W.H. (1999) *The Educator's Guide to Solutioning*. Thousand Oaks, CA: Corwin Press.

Glossary

Active reflection: the active follow-up to reflection - implementation of change

Adult learner: a learner aged over 21

Catastrophizing: where an individual's perception about a situation is that it is much worse than it actually is

Cognitive behavioural approaches: a strategy rooted in a talking therapy, which explores the way in which you think (cognitive) and act (behaviour), breaking down negative patterns and perceptions of thinking and acting

Intrinsic motivation: doing something because it is inherently interesting or enjoyable

Labelling theory: a theory that asks why some people committing some actions come to be defined as deviant, while others do not. Labelling theory is also interested in the effects of labelling on individuals

Massification (of higher education): refers to the period of significant growth in participation rates in HE

Mature learner: a learner aged over 21 and who has had a break in their educational chronology

Political concept: concepts are the tools with which we think, criticize, argue, explain and analyse. Political concepts are building blocks of political understanding: the political world means what our concepts tell us it means

Preconceptions: opinions or conceptions formed in advance of sufficient knowledge or experience, especially a prejudice or bias

Reflection-in-action: frequently described as 'thinking on your feet',
drawing on the previous experiences and learning of the teacher
and applying this in practice at the time of the event

Reflection-on-action: the *conscious act* of reflecting on a situation or
event *after* it has happened, often through replay or documentation

Reframing: the deliberate act of changing the meaning of a situation
or event from a negative to a positive

Schema: a mental or cognitive framework useful for sorting and organ-
izing information in such a way that allows the information to be
understood

Self-actualization: Maslow described self-actualized people as those
who were fulfilled and doing all they were capable of

Self-efficacy: the belief in oneself and one's ability to effect change

Self-reflection: a systemized approach, which can be formal or informal,
of exploring 'what happened' and why

Solution-focused brief approach: a 'can do' approach which focuses on
finding a solution to the problem, as opposed to worrying about
the problem. Adapted from solution-focused brief therapy

Index

TEACHING 14-19
A Handbook

John Bostock and Jane Wood

9780335241910 (Paperback)
January 2012

eBook also available

This book provides a comprehensive overview of how to teach younger learners in Post-Compulsory Education and Training (PCET). With clear guidance and offering practical strategies, *Teaching 14-19* helps you understand how students learn, the theory that supports this and the role of assessment in this process. There is also an extensive focus on how to manage behavior, as this is the most frequently raised concern. The authors show that the overarching models of learning and teaching for 14-19 year olds are very different between school and PCET.

Key features:

- Practical hints, tips and suggestions for practice
- Case studies to help you learn from and reflect on practice
- Discussion of theoretical issues that will enable you to understand and underpin your practice

www.openup.co.uk

OPEN UNIVERSITY PRESS
McGraw - Hill Education